SOFTWARE RELIABILITY MODELLING

SOFTWARE
RELIABILITY
MODELLING

M. Xie

Linkoping University, Sweden

World Scientific

Singapore • New Jersey • London • Hong Kong

Published by

World Scientific Publishing Co. Pte. Ltd.
P O Box 128, Farrer Road, Singapore 9128
USA office: Suite 1B, 1060 Main St., River Edge, NJ 07661
UK office: 73 Lynton Mead, Totteridge, London N20 8DH

Library of Congress Cataloging-in-Publication data is available.

SOFTWARE RELIABILITY MODELLING

ISBN 981-02-0640-2

Printed in Singapore by JBW Printers & Binders Pte. Ltd.

To

all of the teachers and students of
the Special Class of Gifted Young
(the Juvenile Class, the Shao-Nian-Ban)
of the USTC

Preface

According to Professor B.W. Boehm (*Software Reliability Handbook,* ed. P. Rook, Elsevier Applied Science, 1990) the main reasons for a growing world-wide interest in software reliability are the following:

(1) Software is becoming central to many life-critical systems,

(2) Software is created by error-prone humans,

(3) In the real world software is executed by error-intolerant machines,

(4) Software development and maintenance is affected more by budget and schedule concerns than by a concern for reliability.

It is now recognized that many practical problems have arisen due to unreliable or faulty software. In space shuttle programs, aircraft delivery control systems, nuclear power plants and many other areas, the reliability of software is crucial. Software reliability has been an active research area since the early seventies and many software reliability models have been introduced since then.

Many research papers have been published besides the above handbook. The December 1985 and January 1986 *issues of IEEE Transactions on Software Engineering* edited by A. L. Goel and F. B. Bastani were devoted to this problem. *The State of the Art Report: Software Reliability* edited by A. Bendell and P. Mellor (1986), *Software Reliability* edited by B. Littlewood (1987) and the book S*oftware Reliability: Measurement, Prediction, Application* by J. D. Musa et al. (1987) are other recent works. They have also provided inspiration for researchers working on this subject.

Although a great deal of work has been done, there is much more that remains to be studied in software reliability. There has been no systematic publication on software reliability models although there are some internal reports containing models. The aim of this book is to provide interested software engineers and reliability analysts with an overview of the field. Existing models are classified and the most interesting ones are described in detail.

Chapters 1 and 2 are introductory. The first chapter gives an introduction to software reliability and a chronological survey of current software reliability models. In Chapter 2 the classification and unification of the existing models are discussed and some reliability concepts are outlined.

Each of Chapters 3 to 7 concentrates on a different specific model, with one chapter each on the Markov, NHPP, Static, Bayesian and Statistical models. Chapter 3 contains models similar to the Jelinski-Moranda model. NHPP models which are mainly generalizations of the Goel-Okumoto model are studied in Chapter 4. The static models in Chapter 5 are time-independent models, and the Bayesian models discussed in Chapter 6 are models which incorporate prior information for more accurate estimations. Statistical models which include time series models and regression techniques are discussed in Chapter 7.

In Chapter 8 we discuss the problem of determining software release time based on the existing software reliability models. A brief discussion of recent advances related to software reliability engineering issues ends the main part of this book. Finally, there is an extensive list of the most important papers in English on software reliability modelling and its applications. Most of the cited papers can be easily found in the INSPEC data base.

Acknowledgements

It has been an easy choice for me to dedicate this book to the teachers and students of the Special Class of Gifted Young of the University of Science and Technology of China. The academic year 1978–1979 I spent there has given me many unforgettable memories. I would like to express my thanks to all of them for encouraging my search for scientific knowledge. I sincerely wish them a great success.

This book would not have been finished without the help of many of my colleagues and friends. My thanks are due to all of them and especially to Professor Bo Bergman and the members of our department. I am also deeply indebted to those others interested in my research and I especially wish to thank Prof. P. K. Kapur, Prof. T. Khoshgoftaar, Mr. J. D. Musa, Dr. K. Shen, Dr. T. Stålhane, Prof. S. Yamada, Mr. R. Z. Xu, Prof. Y. T. Zhang, Mr. M. Zhao and Mr. O. Åkerlund.

The financial support given to our project on system reliability from CENIIT (CENtre for Industrial Information Technology) at Linköping University has made it possible to finish the book in time. Acknowledgement is also made to STU (Swedish Board for Technical Development) for a previous grant for this project. The staff at the university library are acknowledged for their help with computer searching for literature.

Dr. Phua and Ms. Lee of World Scientific Publishing in Singapore merit special thanks for their interest and assistance that made the publication of this book possible.

Last but not least, I would like to thank my wife Wenhong, who allowed me to spend many nights and weekends working on this book, for her patience and encouragement.

Contents

Some common notations and abbreviations:

$P(A)$ probability of event A
$R(t)$ reliability at time t
$f(t)$ probability density function
$F(t)$ cumulative distribution function

$\lambda(i)$ failure intensity after removing the i:th fault
ϕ the proportionality coefficient of the JM-model
N_0 the number of initial software faults

$N(t)$ The number of faults removed in [0,t]
$\overline{N}(t)$ $N(\infty)-N(t)$, the number of remaining faults at time t
$m(t)$ The expected number of failures in [0,t]
$\lambda(t)$ the failure intensity, defined as the derivative of $m(t)$
τ execution time used in the Musa model

t_i The time between the removing of the (i-1):th and i:th faults,
            or the i:th failure-free time interval
$\tilde{t}$ $\{t_1,t_2,...,t_n; n>0\}$, a set of failure data
$L(\cdot)$ The likelihood function

DFI   Decreasing Failure Intensity
GO   Goel-Okumoto
JM   Jelinski-Moranda
LV   Littlewood-Verrall
NHPP   NonHomogeneous Poisson Process
ROCOF   Rate Of oCcurrence Of Failures

1

Introduction to Software Reliability

Software reliability, as a part of software engineering and reliability analysis, is now an established inter-disciplinary research field. In this chapter we give a brief introduction to software reliability and some other related topics. The importance of software reliability analysis is discussed and some general concepts concerning software reliability are introduced. Then we give a chronological review of the development of software reliability modelling.

1.1. Need for software reliability analysis

Since 1970 researches have been conducted to study the reliability of computer software. As software systems have become more and more complex to design and develop, intensive studies are carried out to increase the chance that software systems will perform satisfactorily in operation. The software crisis is the term people usually use when talking about the problems involved with software products, for example, increasing development cost, lack of the ability to perform an intended task correctly, increasing complexity that makes the software less understandable, etc.

The application of computer systems has now crossed many different fields. Software has become an essential part of many industrial, military and even commercial systems. Both in microcomputers and super-computers we may find programs containing millions of lines of code. This has, together with the application of software in many safety critical systems, led to the fact that software reliability is now an important research area.

Software engineering has been the fastest developing technology during the last century. However, there is no complete, scientific, quantitative measure to assess them. Software reliability measure is one such tool useful for assessing software engineering technologies. As a comparison

1

to hardware development, new technologies have made hardware products relatively reliable and they can be produced at a very low cost. Similar development for software products is desirable.

A software life cycle consists mainly of the following phases, *requirement and specification, design, coding, testing* and *operation/maintenance*. During the testing stage software programs are tested and detected faults are corrected. This is the most important phase of software development because of the high cost associated with it. It is also recognized that the software maintenance cost which is also relatively high, is usually a consequence of the unreliability. Software reliability models are very useful in analysing collected failure data and they are important tools to assess the reliability level reached at the current time.

In order to increase the performance of the software product and to improve the software development process, we must make thorough analyses of the reliability. Reliability assessment methods and improvement techniques have a great value both to software managers and software practitioners. It is also important for software producers as well as for software users.

Methods, such as structural programming, modular programming, fault-tolerance etc., have been widely studied and applied. Other disciplines in software engineering are also developed in order to produce more reliable software. However, no matter how the design and coding of a software product have been made, an important phase during the software development is its testing phase. It is recognized that a great deal of efforts are put down to software testing and the cost of it is one of the major development costs of software products.

It should be stressed here that reliability assessment is not only useful for the software being studied, it has a great value to the future development of other software systems since valuable lessons are learnt and experiences are gained by making quantitative studies of the achieved results. Due to the lack of a systematic analysis of software reliability problems and satisfactory solutions, there is a great need for the study of different models useful in different situations.

Software reliability is an interesting, but difficult, research area. Although there are many software reliability models suggested and studied, none of them are valid at all times and there is no unique model which can perform well for all situations. The reason for this is probably that the assumptions made for each model are correct or are good approximations of the reality just in some situations. Software reliability testing and analysis are not the same as other areas of reliability engineering for which we have a good theoretical support based on statistical methodologies. However, as more researches are carried out in software reliability analysis, it is possible to establish a software reliability theory as we have done for hardware reliability analysis.

1.2. Some general concepts

Because software reliability is a recently developed research field, there are many new concepts introduced in the existing literature. There are also some definitions which are necessary to clarify due to their ambiguousness. In this section we give an introduction to some general concepts concerning software reliability analysis. To begin with, some concepts about software faults and software failures are discussed and we provide some definitions to be used in this book. Then we present a general definition of software reliability and finally the differences between hardware reliability and software reliability are discussed.

1.2.1. Fault and failure

In software reliability literature, different authors use different synonyms referring to software reliability problems, such as fault, error, failure, bug, mistake, malfunction, defect, etc. These terminologies need to be clarified and different concepts have to be unified. We will use the following concepts which have also been commonly accepted.

A software is said to contain a *fault* if, for some input data, the output result is incorrect. Although the definitions of fault are different for different software and different situations, a fault is always an existing part in the software and it can be removed by correcting the erroneous part of the software. By software faults we generally mean all those parts in the software that may cause any problem. Some synonyms used by other authors are error, defect, bug and malfunction. However, we will omit them as far as possible here for the sake of clarity.

For each execution of the software program where the output is incorrect, we observe a software *failure*. A failure may be caused by a software fault or by other reasons, such as human mistakes or hardware failures. For example using wrong input data, incorrect printing of the output result, misinterpretation of the output, etc. may also cause failure. Thus, failure and success are two different possible states of the output. Usually we exclude those failures that are not caused by any software fault, so in this case a failure corresponds to one or more software faults. Hence, if we observe a failure, we can find one or more faults in the software and after correcting those faults, the same failure can not occur again.

Words such as error, bug, mistake, malfunction, defect, etc., are quite ambiguous and will not be used here. Generally, due to human inability to do everything correctly, we do make mistakes. That is we make many errors in designing and coding software programs and even in correcting software faults, we may add new faults into the program by making other mistakes. Usually there are many faults in a software and by running the software program, failures caused by these faults are experienced.

It should be noted here that different users may adopt different definitions of fault and failure due to the implementation of different specifications valid for different applications. These terms are thus strongly user-dependent. However, we will not discuss further about this problem. The definitions will not affect the general methodologies and their applicability. Usually, definitions of faults and failures are obvious in practice by the specification of the software and its intended function.

Generally, during the software testing phase, programs are executed and erroneous outputs are identified. For each incorrect output, we may count it as a failure. Faults that caused the failure are identified and removed. The failure process during the software testing phase may be identified as a fault-removal process. The reliability of the software will be increased during the testing phase as more and more faults are removed. The reliability improvement phenomenon is also called reliability growth.

It is now recognized that no reasonably large software systems are correct in the sense that they always give correct output. Also the size and the complexity of large software packages make it impossible to find and correct all faults. The best one can do is to give the software a reliability requirement and try to meet it by testing the software and correcting detected faults. However, the assessment of the software reliability is not easy. The level of the reliability is usually estimated by using some appropriate models applied to the empirical data from the software failure history.

1.2.2. Definition of software reliability

There are many different measures and definitions of software reliability. A practical one which has been widely used by many software engineers in measuring the quality of software is the number of remaining faults after its release and many models are proposed for the estimation of this quantity. Because the size of software may vary greatly, relative measures such as the number of faults per a given number of codes, are often used in comparing the quality of software.

Due to the fact that not all faults, even those in the same software, have the same rate of occurrence, the number of remaining faults is not a representative measure of the software reliability. A software needs not be more unreliable than another even if it may contain more faults. It is possible for it to be more reliable provided that faults in it have a smaller rate of occurrence. Hence, a probabilistic definition of software reliability should be given. The widely accepted definition is the following.

Software reliability is defined as the probability that the software will be functioning without failure under a given environmental condition during a specified period of time. Here, a software failure means generally the inability of performing an intended task specified by the requirement.

Because software reliability is a probabilistic statement, it is essential to define the condition under which the statement about the reliability of the software is made. The reliability, even for two identical copies of the same software, may be different if they are used under different operational conditions.

The operational condition of the software refers to the environment under which the software is designed to be used. It should be noted that this is usually subjected to great variability. This may vary from one user to another, from one time point to another and from one software to another. Hence, the specification of the operational condition of the software is essential in software reliability assessment.

The time interval under which the software will be used is also important. For a mission it is essential that the software involved will be functioning with an extremely high reliability during a short time interval which is usually much shorter than other phases of software development. For software in commercial applications, the time interval for which the software is designed to be used is much longer and, in this case, we are also interested in the total software cost through the whole software life cycle, because a maintenance is often permitted.

Software reliability, similar to that of hardware, is a time dependent measure which is associated with the distribution of time to failure. Although the software will give a certain output for a certain input, the time to failure has to be treated as a random quantity because it is impossible to predict exactly when the software will fail. It is important to be able to predict and decrease the probability that a failure occurs.

It should be noted that reliability is not the same as correctness. The latter is just a binary condition, but the former is a continuum and can take any value between zero and one. A reliable software is unnecessary to be correct although sometimes software reliability is defined as the probability of correctness. But here the correctness is defined with respect to a given run of the program. However, for a series of runs, a software will eventually fail, since it is certain that a large program does contain a fault.

Other quantities of interests are mean time between failures, failure occurrence rate, distribution of failure free intervals, etc. These are quantities that are receiving more and more attention and many software reliability models have been developed in order to provide tools to estimate them. Further introduction to the mathematical definition of software reliability and other statistical distributions useful in software reliability context will be given in Chapter 2.

1.2.3. Software vs hardware reliability

Software development process is essentially a design process. As causes leading to the failures of software are all due to human errors in creating the software, it may be made perfect without any fault in it. Hence, the software should, theoretically, give correct output for all possible input data. But for hardware systems most failures are caused by some random phenomenon such as the physical aging of the product except some human design errors which are similar to that of software design.

There are many considerable differences between software and hardware systems. Because software reliability theory is strongly influenced by hardware counterpart, it is important to discuss the differences between these two in order to develop realistic models for software purpose. The most significant differences between software and hardware systems which should be identified are the following.

Firstly, software has no *aging property*, i.e. it does not get old like hardware does in the sense that the failure occurrence rate changes due to its own unknown physical aging properties. By keeping the testing intensity constant, software failure intensity is also constant if it has not been subjected to any change. For hardware system, failure probability usually increases due to the wear-out of mechanical elements and this together with a burn-in period in the beginning for which the failure intensity decreases, we usually have a bathtub-shaped failure intensity function.

Secondly, once a software fault is removed from the software, it will never cause the same failure again. In fact, with enough testing effort and by a total testing of all input data which is theoretically finite due to truncation, all software faults can be detected and removed and the software is then perfect. But in practice this is impossible, since it will take millions of years even for a software of moderate size. However, software reliability may be improved by increasing the testing effort and by removing detected faults. For a hardware system, reliability is usually increased by using better material, improved design, increased strength, etc.

Thirdly, copies from a software program are identical. Hence, executions of two copies will give exactly the same results. Commonly defined *redundancy* methodology has no meaning in studying software reliability problems and it is not an applicable tool to increase software reliability. However, software redundancy can be achieved by using other modifications, e.g. multiversion programming technique, but in that case we do not have the same software, and the dependency between one version and another version is a problem that needs to be studied. This may also affect the maintenance of software, so that conventional repair and maintenance policies can not be used for software systems.

Software faults have some deterministic properties. Although the definitions of software faults may depend on particular circumstances, theoretically a fault may be well defined and corrected. Software does not fail due to any unknown reason. In the data-domain, however, an input data will either cause a failure or not, no matter when it is used, because the output will not be changed. However, in the time-domain, we can never say when a software will fail, that is we cannot predict when a software failure will occur in practice. The random nature is due to the unknown locations of faults in the program and the random chosen input data.

The development of hardware reliability has a long history and there are many reliability handbooks which can be used, both for the assessment of the reliability and for the planning of reliability tests. Methods such as fault tree analysis, failure modes and effects analysis, sneak-circuit analysis, etc., have also been developed for hardware reliability purposes. This is another difference between software reliability and hardware reliability, which indicates that the study of software reliability is still at an infant stage.

Historically, software reliability modelling has been strongly influenced by hardware reliability theory. This, on the one hand, has been very helpful in developing software reliability models and analysis methodologies. On the other hand, this makes software reliability strongly connected with hardware reliability theory and this dependence makes it difficult to develop new software reliability technology. Since software is unlike hardware in many aspects, there is a great need to develop new theories, especially for software reliability analysis.

1.3. History of the software reliability

Although software reliability has not been widely studied for a long time, the development of software reliability models has an interesting history. Many different models are proposed, discussed, modified and generalized while some models have also suffered from a lot of critiques. This section briefly reviews the existing software reliability models from a historical point of view. The order of the listed papers is the year when the original and the most significant paper was published internationally. Usually, the results have already been presented at conferences or published as internal reports, so the results seem to be obtained some years before. In addition to the papers introducing new models, there are many good review articles published. Also many papers presenting interesting applications and other experimental results may be found. See Section 1.4 for some literature guide-lines. Previous reviews of the history of software reliability modelling have been published by Schick and Wolverton (1978), Shooman (1984) and Musa et al. (1987a).

1.3.1. Before 1970

Although there are not many papers published internationally, software reliability problems have been discussed during the sixties. It is reasonable to believe that software reliability problems arose already at an early stage of the history of the development of computer systems. However, due to the lack of software reliability concepts and because many problems existed concerning hardware failures, there were not many articles which were directly devoted to software reliability modelling and there was no clear dividing line between software reliability and hardware reliability during this initial period. Here, we will give a brief discussion of some earlier papers related to software reliability analysis.

Weiss (1956) presented some methods for estimating reliability growth in a complex system with Poisson-type failures and many later models are related to the study of reliability growth process. Corcoran et al. (1964) studied a model for estimating reliability after corrective action. Although these models do not directly deal with software reliability analysis the models may be treated as a software reliability model.

Hsugk et al. (1964) presented some experimental results concerning the testing of a switching system in which software was an essential part and contained many programming errors, clerical errors, requirement changes and program improvements. Some histograms of program problems are also shown.

Hudson (1967) observed that software failure process may be described by a Markov birth-death process in which the introduction of faults is a birth process and the removal of faults is a death process. In fact, many later introduced models are general birth-death process models.

Among other earlier papers Sauter (1969) considered some problems in computer programs. Rubey and Harwick (1968) discussed the general problem concerning software quality. There are also many other papers dealing with the proof of the correctness of software, see e.g. London (1969) and other papers cited there.

Although the sixties was not an explosive period of software reliability literature, it is an interesting initial stage for the development of many software reliability models which appeared in different publications in the beginning of the seventies. It is also noted in Shooman (1984) that there are some hardware reliability models which were already used by the end of the sixties and there are several internal reports published within many big industrial companies. Researches done during this period have a significant contribution to the development of software reliability during the seventies.

1.3.2. 1970 - 1979

The development of software reliability theory made its greatest jump at this period during which many software reliability models were introduced and studied. Several important software reliability models were suggested in the beginning of this century. Software reliability analysis which was at the beginning based on the proof of correctness, had passed to a period of stochastic modelling of the failure process and statistical analysis of failure data. Software reliability analysis also earned a recognition among reliability researchers and software practitioners which began to develop models for software reliability purposes. In this section we review most of the earlier models by emphasizing on their influence in later development of software reliability modelling.

Akiyama (1971) made a regression analysis of the failure data for ten software modules where it is observed that there are several factors affecting the number of faults in the software system and this is in fact an early study of using software metrics in reliability prediction.

By assuming that there is a fixed but unknown number of existing faults and the failure intensity is proportional to the number of remaining faults, Jelinski and Moranda (1972) published their famous model for the estimation of the number of initial software faults, using failure data collected during software testing phase. At the same time, Shooman (1972) also published his model similar to that of Jelinski and Moranda and several interesting issues concerning software development cost problems were discussed.

The model by Littlewood and Verrall (1973) which is the first Bayesian software reliability model is another important contribution in the software reliability history. Bayesian methodology in estimating the time between failures of software is studied in that paper.

Schick and Wolverton (1973) suggested two other software reliability models similar to that of Jelinski and Moranda and the differences are that the authors used Rayleigh distribution in modelling time between failures. Also, Wagoner (see e.g. Schick and Wolverton, 1978) studied a similar model by using Weibull distribution. Later Lipow suggested a modification of the Schick-Wolverton model and used grouped data in analysing reliability (see e.g. Schick and Wolverton, 1978).

Another interesting paper is Dickson et al. (1972) which published some results concerning quantitative analyses of software reliability. Some other papers during the earlier seventies are Yourdon (1972) and Coutinho (1973).

Schneidewind (1975) studied the number of faults detected during a given time interval and used a nonhomogeneous Poisson process model with exponentially decreasing intensity function in modelling software failure process. This model seems to be the first of this type and many later models are developed under a nonhomogeneous Poisson process assumption.

Mills (see Schick and Wolverton, 1978), suggested in 1974 a model which introduces a known number of new faults in order to estimate the number of original faults in a computer program. The idea is to adopt a so-called capture-recapture sampling technique in statistics.

A paper which later has had a very strong influence over the development of software reliability is due to Musa (1975). In that paper an execution time theory for the estimation of software reliability is developed and it is suggested that we should use, as a good measure of time for software, the execution time which incorporates test intensity and other program properties.

Moranda (1975) published two other models, called the geometric de-eutrophication process model and the geometric Poisson process model and these models are all modifications of the Jelinski and Moranda model. The main advantage is that the failure intensity decreases faster at the beginning and this is motivated by the fact that earlier detected faults are likely to have higher failure probability.

Trividi and Shooman (1975) suggested a general Markov model in estimating software reliability and the software functioning state is modelled as an up state and failure state as a down state. That is, software testing process is treated as a repair process and the availability may be studied.

By using the idea of the maturity of software, Wall and Ferguson (1977) presented a model connecting the computer time with calender time in studying the analytical relationships between the software maturity and the number of detected faults.

The paper by Forman and Singpurwalla (1977) seems to be the first one to consider the stopping time of software testing and software release policies are studied. Another paper dealing with the same problem is Forman and Singpurwalla (1979) which was published later. Some difficulties of using the Jelinski and Moranda model are identified and some modifications of the estimation procedure are proposed.

In Schick and Wolverton (1978) some models obtained by modifying the Jelinski-Moranda model are presented and in their interesting paper a historical review of the literature may also be found together with a general discussion of some interesting models. The model was originally published in 1973 and some modifications were made, see Goel (1980b) for some interesting discussion of this paper.

Another important paper is due to Lipow (1978) where some software metrics are studied and their correlation with the number of software faults is shown to be successfully used in estimating and predicting the reliability.

A model which has strongly influenced the development of many other models is published in a paper by Goel and Okumoto (1979) where the authors used a simple nonhomogeneous Poisson process model in modelling the software failure process. Many further nonhomogeneous Poisson process models are generalizations and modifications of this simple model which is able to describe software failure process satisfactorily in many cases.

Littlewood (1979b) presented a software reliability model for modular programs in which transfers of control between modules follow a semi-Markov process and this model can be seen as a new whitebox modelling of software reliability.

There are also some other advances of software reliability modelling during the later part of the seventies which can be noted. An imperfect debugging software reliability model has also been studied by Goel, see e.g. Goel (1985). During the same year Nathan (1979) used Gompertz distribution in describing the number of software failures.

1.3.3. 1980 - 1989

During this period of time, many new software reliability models are proposed. Earlier models are also applied to some real data and their drawbacks or imperfections are identified and discussed. The publication of the Musa's software reliability data (see Musa, 1979) has made it possible for many researchers to overcome the difficulty to get relevant software failure data. Due to the large amount of publications, the review here is not at all complete. However, considering the relevancy to software reliability, most of the papers dealing with important new models and related problems are summarized here.

Okumoto and Goel (1980) proposed some software release models and studied optimum release time considering reliability and cost. Thompson and Chelson (1980) studied a Bayesian model in estimating the probability that the software is fault-free and they also developed a decision rule for continuation or termination of testing. An input domain based theory and a derived random walk model for software reliability analysis has been proposed, see e.g. Ramamoorthy and Bastani (1982). Cheung (1980) studied a user-oriented software reliability model which is based on the reliabilities of individual modules and the measured inter-modular transition probabilities as the user profile.

Shanthikumar (1981) presented a general Markov model with state and time dependent transition rates and provided a binomial distribution model of the number of remaining faults. An extension of the Jelinski and Moranda model involving more parameters and hence more flexible is presented in Moranda (1981). Littlewood (1981) developed a model for the fault-removal process using a Bayesian differential debugging model and the model is applicable both to software reliability growth and to hardware reliability growth by eliminating errors. A quasi-Bayes model for estimating software reliability growth is proposed in Higgins and Tsokos (1981).

Software complexity reliability models have been studied in Ottenstein (1981) and Schneider (1981) who presented some empirical models using some software complexity metrics. Also software fault-seeding models have been studied in Duran and Wiorkowski (1981) where the authors clarified the model originally proposed previously by Mill in the seventies.

Statistical prediction techniques have been proposed to be used in analysing software reliability failure data by Dale and Harris (1982). Castillo and Sieworek (1982) presented a software reliability prediction model considering workload. Trachtenberg (1982) used Rayleigh distribution in modelling the failure rate of the software and his argument was that the number of faults found is proportional to the number of man-hours worked. Lipow (1982) presented some models to estimate the number of faults per line of code which is a kind of complexity measure.

Many papers dealing with the choice among different software reliability models have also been published in the beginning of the eighties. Model comparisons have been studied in the papers by Littlewood (1980b), Keiller et al. (1983), Musa and Okumoto (1983).

Nonhomogeneous Poisson process models have now, at this stage, attacted more attention by many software engineers and researchers. Goel (see e.g. Goel, 1985) generalized the Goel-Okumoto model by adding a third parameter that reflects the quality of the test, see Goel (1985). Ohba et al. (1982) presented a model using a nonhomogeneous Poisson process with S-shaped mean value function. Some interesting results using nonhomogeneous Poisson process models are also presented in Yamada et al. (1983) by observing that software reliability growth curve is often S-shaped. Yamada and Osaki (1983b) studied a software reliability growth model by assuming different types of software errors. These Japanese researchers made later further progress in studying the various S-shaped nonhomogeneous Poisson process models.

Meinhold and Singpurwalla (1983) developed some Bayesian software reliability models and it is pointed out that some alternative models can be obtained by assigning specific prior distributions to the parameters in the Jelinski-Moranda model. Using martingale theory Koch and Speij (1983) derived the posterior distribution of the number of remaining faults and several earlier models can also be derived using special prior distributions.

Kremer (1983) formulated software failure process as a general birth-death process and obtained some general results. Kubat and Koch (1983a) presented some procedures useful to manage testing effectiveness. In another paper Kubat and Koch (1983b) investigated some different test protocols to measure software reliability based on the Jelinski and Moranda model.

A software release model is presented in Koch and Kubat (1983) where a decision procedure to determine an optimum release time is discussed. Another application of software reliability model in deciding optimum release time is presented in Shanthikumar and Tufekci (1983).

Ohba (1984) studied some particular nonhomogeneous Poisson process models such as the delayed S-shaped growth model, the inflection S-shaped model and the hyper-exponential model. Musa and Okumoto (1984b) continued their studies by suggesting a logarithmic Poisson model based on the execution time theory. Due to the similarity of software faults and hardware design faults, Littlewood (1984) discussed the application of the Duane model of reliability growth which has been widely used for repairable systems.

A Fourier series model is developed in Crow and Singpurwalla (1984) which is another methodology to describe failure data and this model can successfully be used in predicting future behaviour of the failure process, especially for the cases when a clustering of failures occurs. Huang (1984), (1985) studied a hypergeometric distribution model for estimating the number of software faults based on a model originally proposed by Mill during the seventies.

The comparison of software reliability models, which is very essential for being able to chose a good model, is studied in a joint paper by Iannino, Musa, Okumoto and Littlewood (1984) where a set of criteria are proposed.

Bayesian extensions of existing software reliability models have interested more and more researchers. In a paper published by Langberg and Singpurwalla (1985) some Bayesian formulations of the Jelinski and Moranda model and a unification of some of the earlier models is suggested.

In December 1985 "IEEE Transaction on Software Engineering" published a special issue on software reliability edited by A.L. Goel and F.B. Bastani. This is the only one of two parts with the second part published in the January issue of 1986. Both contain many high-quality papers while several new models may also be found.

Jewell (1985) extended a result by Langberg and Singpurwalla (1985) and made a further extension of the Jelinski-Moranda model. Ross (1985b) studied an additive failure rate model and presented some theoretical results on the stopping rule problem. Singpurwalla and Soyer (1985) presented some Kalman filter models for software reliability analysis. Downs (1985) published two software reliability models with parameters depending on the number of paths and the number of the paths affected by each fault. The problem of increasing software reliability by using fault-tolerance techniques such as multiversion programming is studied in Avizienis (1985), Anderson et al. (1985) and Eckhardt and Lee (1985). Each paper contains many previous references in this area.

Exponential order statistic models in studying software reliability growth are discussed in Miller (1986) and many existing models can be derived as special cases of this general framework. A discrete model based on independent multinomial trials and a continuous model based on the order statistics of independent nonidentical exponential random variables are examined in Scholz (1986). Sumita and Masuda (1986) developed a new hardware-software reliability model formulated as a multivariate stochastic process.

Crow (1986) discussed reliability growth potential and presented a method for assessing software reliability parameter based on random sampling of the input space. Bendell (1986) introduced the use of exploratory data analysis technique for assessing software reliability. Some particular models discussed are time series analysis and proportional hazards modelling. Regression models are also discussed in Ascher (1986).

In a series of papers, Yamada and his co-authors studied a testing-effort dependent reliability model, see e.g. Yamada et al. (1986b). In their papers, models for determining optimum software release policy are also considered, see also Yamada and Osaki (1986) and references there in. Kenett and Pollak (1986) considered a general semi-parametric model for reliability growth testing. Sumita and Shanthikumar (1986) presented another Markov model which takes into account the fact that more than one fault may be removed or inserted.

The State of the Art Report edited by Bendell and Mellor (1986) is another source of collection of research work. Chan (1986a) presented some adaptive models in predicting software reliability. A framework for software reliability modelling is suggested in Gray (1986) where statistical theory of point processes is used. Hamer (1986) discussed the relation between software reliability and some existing software metrics. Soyer (1986) reviewed some time series models for describing software failures and studied some inferential procedures.

An important progress of software reliability modelling is the publication of the book by Musa et al. (1987a). An elementary and practical description of software reliability analysis is discussed. Although there are some books on software reliability technology published earlier, this is the first book discussing software reliability modelling and related topics.

Schagen and Sallin (1987) studied a logistic model for fitting software failure data. Levendel (1987) developed a model considering fault detection and fault removal. Hamlet (1987) proposed a theory of "probable correctness" to assess software reliability through testing.

Xie (1987) derived two Markov process models by generalizing the Jelinski-Moranda model which is modified by assuming that an earlier detected fault contributes more to the total failure rate. A general version of the Markov model is also presented in Xie and Bergman (1988). Bittanti et al. (1988b) presented a similar model generalizing that of Jelinski and Moranda.

Mazzuchi and Soyer (1988) showed that the Littlewood-Verrall model is an empirical Bayes model and they presented some fully Bayes models called Bayes Empirical-Bayes model. Wright and Hazelhurst (1988) concentrated on the modelling of the failure rate until next failure in overcoming some difficulties in the Jelinski and Moranda model. Weiss and Weynker (1988) generalized the Nelson model and presented an extended domain-based model for software reliability.

Ohba and Chou (1989) suggested some generalizations of existing software models considering the possibility of imperfect debugging. An interesting error complexity software reliability model is proposed in Nakagawa and Hanata (1989). Tohma et al. (1989a) studied a new model in estimating the number of the remaining faults using a hypergeometric distribution. Brown et al. (1989) presented a probabilistic model which determines the optimum number of test cases.

Kubat (1989) proposed a stochastic model for describing the behaviour of modular software and derived the system failure rate under some general assumptions. Some optimum release policies for modular software have been studied in Masuda et al. (1989).

Littlewood and Miller (1989) presented a conceptual methodology in modelling software reliability in multiversion software and the original model is due to Eckhardt and Lee (1985). Stålhane (1989) presented a general Markov model for usage dependent software reliability analysis. Joe (1989) discussed a general order statistics model and studied some inference problems.

1.3.4. 1990 - present

At present, a deep insight has been opened. Software reliability modelling is considered as a part of software quality and software engineering. A bridge between software engineers and statistical methodists has been built although the gap between practitioners and theoreticians is still waiting to be filled. Furthermore, it seems that software reliability models have been saturated in the literature already by the end of the eighties. Many new models are either generalizations of older models or special cases of existing models.

Many software reliability researchers are now also working on other related problems such as multiversion programming, software tolerance modelling, software metrics modelling. Some progress may be identified already. The following can be noted and most of them can also be considered as new research directions in the near future.

Levendel (1990) presented a birth-death model considering the defect detection, the defect removal and the factor of introduction of new faults due to imperfect removal of defects. In Brocklehurst et al. (1990) a technique called recalibration is presented in detail and it is shown to be a useful to improve reliability prediction and the essential part is the u-plot developed by Littlewood and his colleagues.

Levin and Yadid (1990) developed a model useful for determining an optimum release time for releasing new versions of a program package. Petrova and Veevers (1990) discussed some reliability concepts and studied the use of non-stochastic-based metrics in quantification of software reliability. Christodoulakis and Panziou (1990) presented a software reliability prediction methodology using optimum estimation model.

Ashrafi et al. (1990) presented a decomposition software reliability model in which the software system is decomposed into subsystems. Munson and Khoshgoftaar (1990a) studied regression modelling of software quality.

Fault-tolerance is a widely used technique to increase the reliability of computer systems. Fault-coverage is the important measure of the effectiveness of these techniques. Balakrishnan and Raghavendra (1990) studied a fault-tolerance model and derived some new results and other references may be found in that paper. Seth et al. (1990) developed a relation between the average fault coverage and circuit testability. Although the paper is not specifically for software reliability, it contains some interesting results in discussing fault coverage of a test and detection probability of a fault.

Wohlin and Körner (1990) studied a software reliability model by modelling the spreading, detection and costs of software failures. A general theory considering software average error size, apparent error density and workload is developed by Trachtenberg (1990) and some existing models are developed as a special case using this general model. Selby (1990) used an empirical analysis of failure data to evaluate software reliability.

Bayesian software reliability analysis has recently been studied in Becker and Camarinopoulos (1990) where the authors proposed a new model of a possibly correct software. Also Csenki (1990) derived some theoretical results using an existing Bayesian software reliability model.

Cost-benefit analysis has recently been studied in Keene (1991), Chenoweth (1991) and Vienneau (1991). A procedure for reliability demonstration testing for discrete-type software products is studied in Sandoh and Sawada (1991).

Some new models and research results are presented at the first international conference on software reliability engineering. Shooman (1991) presented a new micro software reliability model by considering the module testing phase, integration testing phase and field operation in order to improve the prediction. A model which is an equally weighted linear combination of some different models has been proposed and studied by Lyu and Nikora (1991). Based on a continuous time Markov model, the reliability performance modelling of N version programming is studied by Goseva-Popstojanova and Grnarov (1991).

1.4. Bibliographic notes

There are many survey papers that can be read at an introductory stage. Interested readers are referred to the review papers by Ramamoorthy and Bastani (1982), Shooman (1984), Musa (1984), Goel (1985), Yamada and Osaki (1985c), Lipaev (1987) and Mazzuchi and Singpurwalla (1988).

In Schick and Wolverton (1978) earlier history of software reliability modelling and analysis may be found. Shanthikumar (1983) reviewed several software reliability models. The report by Stålhane (1986) summarized 56 software reliability models prior to 1986 and a chronological review is also provided.

Other general papers discussing software reliability models and related topics are Amster and Shooman (1975), Littlewood (1979a), (1980b), Musa (1980), Misra (1983), Yamada and Osaki (1983a), Cavano (1984), Hsia (1984), Iannino et al. (1984), Barlow and Singpurwalla (1985), Mellor (1987b), Downs (1986), Bittanti et al. (1988a), O'Connor (1988), Dudley (1988), Bastani and Ramamoorthy (1989), Brocklehurst et al. (1990) and Bergman and Xie (1991), Keene (1991b) and Keiller and Miller (1991).

The book *"Software Reliability: Measurement, Prediction, Application"* by Musa et al. (1987a), *"the State of the Art Report: Software Reliability"* edited by Bendell and Mellor (1986), *"Software Reliability"* edited by Littlewood (1987a) and *"Software Reliability Handbook"* edited by Rook (1990) are also good reference books containing many interesting results.

Several special issues of special interests are

Special issue on "Software Reliability", in *Journal of Systems and Software*, Vol.1, No.1, 1980;
Special issues on "Software Reliability", part 1, in *IEEE Transaction on Software Engineering*, Vol.SE-11, No.12, 1985;
Special issue on "Software Reliability", part 2, in *IEEE Transaction on Software Engineering*, Vol.SE-12, No.1, 1986;

Special issue on "Software Quality Assurance", in *Information and Software Technology*, Vol.32, No.1, 1990;
Special issue on "Software Reliability and Metrics", in *Software Engineering Journal*, Vol.5, No.1, 1990;
Special issue on Fault-Tolerant Computing, in *IEEE Transaction on Computers*, Vol.C-16, No.2, 1990;
Special issue on "Software Fault-tolerance", in *IEEE Transaction on Selected Topics in Communications*, Vol.STC-8, No.2, 1990;
Special issue on "Software Reliability and Safety", in *Reliability Engineering and System Safety*, Vol.32, No.1, 1991.

Also many issues in *IEEE Transaction on Reliability* contain a section "Software Reliability" where many interesting papers can be found.

There are also a great number of proceedings of international conferences where many interesting papers may be found, for example:

Advances of Reliability Technology Symposium,
Annual Reliability and Maintainability Symposium,
International Computer Software and Applications Conference,
International Conference on Fault-Tolerant Computing Systems,
International Conference on Software Engineering,
International Symposium on Software Reliability Engineering,
Society of Software Engineers Symposium - Scandinavian Chapter,

All of the papers referred to in Section 1.3 are completely listed in the references at the end of this book.

2

Elements of Software Reliability Modelling

In this chapter we give a brief introduction to software reliability modelling and some other related statistical concepts. First some classification systems of the existing software reliability models are presented and some unifications of them are discussed. Here, we mainly discuss the classification of the existing models according to the probabilistic assumptions made concerning the software failure process. Other classification systems will only be briefly mentioned. In Section 2.2 we discuss the differences between fault-counting models and failure intensity estimation models which should be identified in developing new models for the analysis of software reliability. Some commonly used assumptions and their realism are discussed in Section 2.3. Finally, we review some reliability theoretical results which are useful in studying software reliability models.

2.1. Classification and unification of the existing models

In Section 1.3 a historical review of many existing software reliability models is presented from which it can be seen that there are many models suggested and studied while some are more widely discussed than others. If we consider their assumptions and their applicabilities, many models are also very similar. In order to distinguish these models from each other and to make comparison of any two models, suitable classifications are very useful. Due to the variety of the existing models this is not an easy task and several different classification systems have been suggested in many papers. Some unifications of the existing models are also proposed in the literature by several authors. The classification which will be used in this book is first presented. A brief description of other classification systems which are useful in different contexts is also provided together with the references where the original classification may be found.

2.1.1. A classification according to probabilistic assumptions

In this section we discuss the classification problem of software reliability models. We propose a classification system which will be used in this book. It is according to this classification that we will present some typical models in later chapters.

For any software reliability model there are usually several assumptions on the software failure detection rates, the location of faults in the data space, the number of faults in the software, the condition of the test environment etc. involved. A classification may be based on the probabilistic assumptions made in the models. Classifying models according to their assumptions can be helpful in dividing models into separated classes and it provides some insights to obtain new models which are more realistic than the existing ones by identifying the unrealistic assumptions made for these existing models.

A stochastic process is usually incorporated in the description of the failure phenomenon, such as the Markov process assumption, nonhomogeneous Poisson process assumptions which are widely used. Some other models deal mainly with the inference problems based on the failure data and these models include Bayesian models and other statistical methods. There are several static models not taking the dynamic aspect of the failure process into consideration, such as input-domain-based models, seeding and tagging models and software complexity models which will also be discussed in this book.

Markov models:

A model belongs to this class if its probabilistic assumption of the failure counting process is essentially a Markov process, usually a birth-death process. The main characteristic of such a model is that the software, at a given point of time, has a countably many states and such states may be the number of the remaining faults. Given that the process is at a specific state, its future development does not depend on its past history and the transition probabilities among these states depend only on the present state of the software. The failure intensity of the software is assumed to be a discontinuous function which depends on the current state of the software. In Chapter 3 typical models using such Markov formulation of the failure process are presented. Note that in this group of models we also count those Markov models in a system context, that is Markov models which use the structure of the software system.

Nonhomogeneous Poisson process models:

A model is classified as a nonhomogeneous Poisson process model if the main assumption is that the failure process is described as a nonhomogeneous Poisson process. The class of nonhomogeneous Poisson process models is widely used in studying hardware reliability growth in design processes. They can be directly adopted in software reliability analysis due to the similarity of software and hardware reliability growth. The main characteristic of this type of models is that there is a mean value function which is defined as the expected number of failures up to a given time. For different choices of this mean value function we have different models which may be used in different situations. Some typical nonhomogeneous Poisson process models are presented in Chapter 4.

Bayesian models:

Usually some interesting information about the software to be studied is available before the testing starts and it can be used in combination with the collected test data to make a more accurate estimation and prediction of the reliability. Bayesian analysis is a commonly accepted technique to incorporate previous knowledge and hence it is a helpful tool in analysing software failure data. There are many models using Bayesian methodology in studying software reliability problems and in making decisions based on the collected software failure data. Typical existing Bayesian models are discussed in Chapter 6. Bayesian models here include all such models for which a Bayesian assumption or a Bayesian analysis method is adapted.

Statistical data analysis methods:

An essential problem in studying software reliability is that of prediction. Different statistical models and methods can be applied for the analysis of software failure data. This class of models here includes time series models, proportional hazards models, regression models, exploratory data analysis etc. The existing models using these techniques are briefly reviewed in Chapter 7.

Input-domain-based models:

There are many models that do not make any dynamic assumption of the failure process. One of these is the input-domain-based models which considers the software input space from which test cases are chosen. The studied quantity is the probability that a randomly chosen input datum according to the operational usage of the software will lead to a failure. By recording the output results from a series of test cases, this probability can be estimated using some statistical sampling techniques.

Seeding and tagging models:

Another type of models for the estimation of software reliability is by using the so-called seeding and tagging model which is a statistical technique called the capture-recapture method. Some models are developed for this purpose. The general idea is that some known number of software faults are injected or seeded into the software and after the testing, we detect a number of faults in which some are seeded. Knowing the portion of the seeded faults, the total number of inherent software faults can then be estimated.

Software metrics models:

A software metric is usually a measure of the software complexity which is very useful in estimating and allocating software development efforts. It is obvious that a larger or more complex software also contains more faults than others. Software metrics can thus be used in estimating the number of software faults in the software. There are many such models developed and although most of them are empirical results, they are very useful at earlier stages of the software development.

For the last three groups of models, no dynamic assumption is necessary. Since the most essential attribute of those models is the number of faults, they are of limited applicability in reliability context. There is a need to transform the number of faults to the dynamic reliability by incorporating test intensity, fault-occurrence rate etc. Also the estimation from those models is very rough and the estimates are often not sufficiently accurate. However, due to their applicability in other areas of software engineering, especially in estimating and allocating software development resources at an earlier stage, they are briefly discussed in Chapter 5.

2.1.2. Other classification systems

Model classifications are useful in identifying similarity of different models and they provide ideas in choosing an appropriate model. The existing software reliability models can be classified in many different ways. There are several classification systems proposed by various authors in the literature. Some of them are also quite similar and all of them are useful in different contexts.

Ramamoorthy and Bastani (1982) divided the existing models according to the phase of the software development where the model is the most applicable. That is, a model can be classified as a debugging phase model, validation phase model, operational phase model and maintenance phase model. However, most of the models are mainly applicable during the testing phase which is also the most important phase of software development with respect to software reliability. With some modification, many models can directly be applied to other phases of the software development, such as the operation phase.

Another classification theme according to the nature of the debugging strategy is also presented in Bastani and Ramamoorthy (1986). Generally, the models used for assessing software reliability based on earlier failure history are called software reliability growth model, since the testing and debugging increase the reliability and the process is a reliability growth process. Another class of models which is called sampling models, deals with input data selection. Finally, a third class of models is called seeding models and it assumes that a given number of faults are inserted into the software and the reliability is estimated by using the numbers of detected inherent faults and seeded faults.

Software reliability growth models may also be divided into fault-counting models and non-fault-counting models according to whether the reliability is expressed as the number of faults or not, see e.g. Bastani and Ramamoorthy (1986). A fault-counting model estimates both the number of remaining faults and the occurrence rate of the next failure. Another model characteristic which may be used to distinguish many models, is their probabilistic assumptions of the failure intensity which may be deterministic, stochastic or Bayesian. Also different classification systems may be combined to divide models into smaller groups.

Goel (1985) divided the existing models into four groups: times between failures models, failure count models, fault seeding models and input domain based models. If the times between failures are studied, the model is called a times between failures model. Most of Markov models presented in Chapter 3 are times between failures models according to this classification. Failure count models deal mainly with the number of failures in a specified time interval. All nonhomogeneous Poisson process models in Chapter 4 belong to this group. If a number of faults are seeded and a capture-recapture technique is used in modelling and testing the software, then this model is called fault seeding model. Finally, input domain based models estimate the correctness of an execution of the software using the failures observed during execution of the test cases sampled from the input space.

Musa (1984) discussed the possibility of classifying the models in terms of different attributes. An example is the time domain used for the models, that is whether the calender time or the execution time is adapted. Only a few existing models explicitly assume that the execution time is the underlying time measure. However, for any dynamic model, execution time can be incorporated and the probabilistic nature of the model assumptions is not changed.

Another interesting classification proposed by Musa (1984) is to divide models into different classes according to whether the number of failures that can occur is finite or not. The finite failure category includes those models making the assumption that there are a finite number of faults in the software and the number of faults is an important attribute while the infinite failure category includes those models not making such an assumption. Hence, for an infinite failure category model an infinite number of faults may exist in the software. The underlying distribution of time between failures may then be combined with these two classes to further classify some existing models in Musa (1984).

Another classification system has been used in Mellor (1987b) where a family tree is presented. Existing models are divided into blackbox models and structure models according to whether the software structure is used in studying software reliability and modelling the failure process or not. Structure models are further divided into inter-failure time models and fault manifestation models. However, according to Mellor (1987b), most existing dynamic stochastic models are exponential order statistic models which may be seen as a kind of unification of many models.

Although there are many different classifications of existing software reliability models, most of them are very similar. We will in this book classify the models into the classes discussed in the previous section. It has been pointed out by other authors that almost all of the existing models can be used, with some minor modifications, for the different time domain. They are also applicable to different phases of software life cycle such as testing phase, maintenance phase. Readers interested in other classifications, such as those discussed above, are referred to other review papers.

2.1.3. Unification of some existing models

There are many software reliability models which are generalizations of earlier ones in a wide sense. Many models developed can be unified under some general formulation. Model unification is very useful for the study of general models without making many assumptions. Here, we mainly discuss the generalized order statistics models and Bayesian formulations of software reliability models which have appeared in several papers.

It has been pointed out by various authors that the class of general order statistic models is one of the general classes of software reliability models. Many existing models can be obtained by using appropriate assumptions of the underlying statistical distribution of times between failures. For general order statistic models, times of discovering faults are assumed to be order statistics from a sample of unknown size from a distribution which belongs to a parametric family. Exponential order statistics model and Weibull order statistics model are some examples. For a general discussion, see Miller (1986). Order statistic models have also been considered in Mellor (1987b) as a general class of models which contains many existing models.

A unification using Bayesian formulation of the Jelinski-Moranda model is provided by Langberg and Singpurwalla (1985). For example, NHPP models can be derived from general order statistics models by assuming the number of faults to be a Poisson random variable. Their conclusion is that the Jelinski-Moranda model which is the simplest order statistics model is the central one of software reliability models.

There are some other model unification schemes in the existing literature, although most of them are in fact similar unifications of dynamic models. Stålhane (1989) presented a general approach to the modelling of the software failure process. The general framework is based on the assumption that the fault-occurrence process assumed to be Markov, depends on another process called execution process which is assumed to be nonhomogeneous Poisson. The failure time distribution may depend on the random usage condition and the uncertainty of the location of faults in the program. Some different models can be treated as special cases of this general model.

Trachtenberg (1990) made another attempt to unify some commonly discussed models. By assuming that software failure rates are the product of software average fault size, apparent fault density and workload, a general theory is presented. Several existing dynamic models are also derived as special cases of this general theory.

2.2. Fault counting vs failure intensity modelling

Most existing models contain a parameter which represents the number of initial faults in the software. If the number of faults is assumed to be finite, then attention is usually focused on the estimation of the number of remaining faults. This is due to the historical development of trying to construct a fault-free software package and the practical simplicity of just counting the number of failures occurred. As we noted before, attempts have been made, at an earlier period of software development history, in searching for analytical methods to prove the correctness of software which is almost impossible for software of moderate size.

The number of faults is usually not a representative measure of software reliability. A program may contain many faults, each with a very low rate of occurrence and such a program can be more reliable than another one which contains fewer faults but each with a high rate of occurrence. Hence, the total rate of failure occurrence, that is the failure intensity of the program, is more important to be measured and studied in the context of software reliability analysis.

The software fault-removal process is a kind of repair process. Software reliability models which are mainly applicable during the testing phase are also models for repairable systems. Failure intensity function which is associated with repairable systems is usually much more interesting than the number of software faults. This is the reason why many hardware reliability models such as nonhomogeneous Poisson process models are applicable here.

Estimating the current failure intensity is not an easy task in general, although for many simple dynamic models an estimate can be directly obtained. Besides the number of faults, the failure intensity in testing depends on many different factors such as the test intensity, the homogeneity of the software testing, etc. and the failure intensity in operation varies even more from a case to another. It is important to use models which are able to incorporate these factors. However, further assumptions on the testing process are usually needed to get a mathematically tractable model.

As discussed before, models may be classified to fault count models and failure intensity estimation models. It is important to study the latter type of models on which attention will also be focused in this book. It should be noted here that if the failure intensity can be related to the number of faults, then the number of existing faults may be used to predict reliability. However, this relation has to be determined and this is usually not easy and as discussed before, there are many other factors affecting the reliability.

2.3. Limitations of some common assumptions

In order to obtain a useful model, further assumptions about the fault-detection and fault-removal process are needed. In this section we discuss the limitations of some commonly used assumptions and present some possibilities of modifying the failure data so that these assumptions are satisfied.

2.3.1. The size of a fault

Many software reliability models, especially several earlier models, assume that all software faults are of the same size. This implies that each fault contributes the same amount to the software failure probability. By removing a software fault, the reliability is increased. By this assumption, however, no matter which of the remaining faults is removed, the reliability of the software will increase by the same amount.

This is one of the most critical assumptions of many models and it has been widely discussed because in practice this is never true. For all software, there are some faults which are more frequently encountered than others due to the fact that they contribute more to the failure probability of the software than other faults do. The reason may just be that they cause more data in the input space to fail and hence they can be detected easier. The failures may also have more serious consequences and testing effort has been concentrated on finding them. Another reason may be that they are just easier to be detected due to the reason that similar faults have occurred many times before.

Although the assumption that all software faults are of the same size is not realistic, it is not easy to replace it by a more realistic one. The definition of the size of a fault is also ambiguous. In reliability context, it should be the probability of detecting it which is equivalent to the contribution to the failure intensity by the fault. However, this can not be measured and this is just what we try to estimate in practice. More practically the size of a fault may be defined by measures such as the number of lines affected by the fault. Another possible measure of the size of a fault may be the number of the input data causing failure due to this fault. Also the size of a fault may even be defined as the seriousness of the failure caused by the fault.

If the assumption that all faults are of equal size is used, then the prediction of the number of remaining faults is usually optimistic. This may be explained by the fact that there are usually much more remaining faults than estimated, each with a much smaller size than the detected ones since the remaining faults are not as easily detected.

Even though it is commonly recognized that not all faults are of the same size, measures of the sizes of faults have not been much studied and this is a topic for further research. However, it has been observed, see e.g. Bishop et al. (1987), that the failure occurrence rate of faults is approximately exponentially distributed. If the testing is completely random and the failure occurrence rate is proportional to the number of input data that will cause a failure, then the number of input data affected by a fault can be approximated by geometric distribution which is the discrete counterpart of the exponential distribution.

In order to remove the assumption that all faults are of the same size, many authors have proposed new models for which more reasonable assumptions are made. But usually more parameters are involved in these models and the applicability is then limited because of the increased complexity. In practice, it is important for a model to be simple and although an assumption is not fully realistic, any model which gives a good estimate of the failure intensity is worth considering.

2.3.2. Random and homogeneous testing

Most existing models assume that the testing is performed completely homogeneously and randomly, that is the test data are chosen from the input space of the software by some random mechanism and the software is tested using these data during some homogeneous condition. This is another drawback of many software reliability models because in practical situations, this is not the case.

Usually testing is not completely homogeneous due to many practical reasons such as holidays, sickness, availability of testing facility, etc. Also the test data are not randomly chosen; they are usually chosen in order to increase the testing effectiveness, that is to detect more faults by using a smaller number of data. Many existing software reliability models are made useless because of these reasons.

In practice, it is important to deal with the case of nonhomogeneous testing. An important step in this direction was taken by Musa (1975) where the author presented a model using execution time instead of calender time as a measure of time for software systems. Generally, it has been shown that testing is usually more homogeneous with respect to execution time than calender time. However, many models can be slightly modified and applied to other time units and execution time component can also be incorporated.

In order to deal with the case of non-random testing, it should be noted that an important goal is to have an estimate of the reliability of the software after release. It is therefore important that tested input data are chosen as similar as possible to the real world situation, which has also become a common situation. If this is the case, the failure intensity during operation can be related to the failure intensity during testing by a factor which may be interpreted as the intensity of execution.

It should be pointed out here that the failure process is strongly affected by the testing strategy used. If a non-random testing strategy, such as unit testing, module testing, has been applied this should be taken into consideration. In order to use a good reliability model we should incorporate the testing strategy into our reliability model as far as possible. It is obvious that the best model may vary from time to time and differ from software to software.

There are several other factors which affect the homogeneity of software testing worth considering. Usually, testing has already started at the time when the software is not completely coded. Also, module testing of a software is a common situation. In that case, one should carefully divide the failure data and make use of other available information. The estimates of the reliability of different modules should be combined and a white-box model, that is a model using the structure of the software, should be used.

2.3.3. Estimation vs prediction

Usually, having an estimate of the current reliability of the software is not a final goal. It is essential for a software manager to be able to predict the future behaviour of the software failures. The prediction is important for the allocation of further testing resources and for the study of software release problems.

In order to make an accurate prediction of the failure behaviour, the condition under which a test is carried out has to be considered. By using different test strategies we may get different test data and different results may be obtained. The problems in the previous section are usually the reason that many models fail to produce acceptable prediction of the failure process.

It is commonly assumed that the testing is performed under a condition completely identical to that in the usage. In that case, the estimated current reliability during the testing is also the reliability just after the release. However, testing is usually carried out under more serious condition so that more faults are likely to be detected in a short period of time. As software reliability depends strongly on the concentration of the input data in the input space, it happens that some increase of the failure probability occurs just after the software release which can be explained by the fact that the testing has been concentrated on another region of the input space than the reality.

Sometimes a simple factor relating the condition of testing and that during operation exists. For example, sometimes it happens during the testing, that the intensity of execution of the software is higher while during the usage, the intensity is reduced by a constant factor. If this is the case, the estimated failure intensity may easily be transformed to the failure intensity during the operation.

2.3.4. Blackbox vs whitebox models

A software reliability model can be obtained by treating the software as a blackbox and trying to fit the failure data by an analytical expression. Such a model does not require any knowledge of the software structure. It describes the failure time by a probability distribution which is different for different software and different testing environments and the reliability is solely estimated, based on the failure history.

This way of modelling software reliability, which often gives unacceptable estimate of software reliability, has been criticized by many authors. For a software engineer, the structure of the software is completely known. There is a great deal of information available and it should be utilized in order to give an accurate estimate of the reliability. It may be arguable that the software is usually a whitebox which means that its internal structure may be observed.

Traditionally, there are some studies carried out in order to prove the correctness of the software. Using all available information of the software, the software can, theoretically, be made fault-free. This way of modelling may be treated as pure whitebox modelling. However, the goal of a fault-free software can hardly be achieved with any reasonable amount of testing effort and for a reasonably large software. In general, pure whitebox models are not very applicable and some simplification has to be made.

There are some models, such as the input-domain-based models, suggested by studying the test coverage of the test data and the reliability may be estimated by the part of the software input space which is covered by testing. A whitebox model can, theoretically, be derived by studying the test cases and their impact on the software input space. However, a complete whitebox model is difficult to be obtained. Usually, some abstraction must be made and many assumptions have to be used in order to get a mathematical tractable model.

There are several models using the modular structure of the software. Such a model should be treated as a "grey-box" model since it uses a part of information about the software. There are some other possibilities of utilizing information about the software. For example, information can be incorporated into the models using Bayesian analysis, regression analysis or software complexity models.

As a general conclusion, a model should be made as white as possible, but this is not easy because of many practical difficulties. However, blackbox models are also very useful and important, mainly due to the reason that deterministic causes of unreliability should be eliminated by using improved reliability technology and software quality control tools. Random testing will then be an important method to assess software reliability level as it is for many hardware systems.

2.4. Some reliability theoretical concepts and notations

Software reliability modelling is now an established research area of reliability analysis whose theory can be found in many standard text books. Here, we will only review some concepts and notations which are frequently used in this book. Note that in this section we only consider the nonrepairable case. We are interested in the time to next failure and the probability distribution of this random quantity. Time should be treated as the local time, such as the time since last failure. In reliability engineering, we usually deal with failure-free time intervals, that are nonnegative random variables. In this section we consider only so-called *life distributions*. A distribution F(t) is called life distribution if it satisfies the following condition

$$F(t) = 0 \ \ for \ all \ t{<}0.$$

2.4.1. Some important reliability measures

Although software reliability is a new discipline, hardware reliability has been studied for a long time. Software reliability is also strongly influenced by hardware reliability theory, as the definition of the software reliability is similar to that of hardware. Generally, the reliability of a software, R(t), is defined as

R(t) = probability that the software will be functioning without failure under a given environmental condition during time [0,t).

It should be noted that software systems and hardware systems are different, see e.g. Section 1.2.3 for some discussions concerning this. For software, the environmental condition is not the same as that for hardware and neither their failure causes nor failure consequences are the same.

However, the probabilistic definitions are identical and hence the theories of probability and statistics to be used are also similar.

Denote by T the random failure-free time interval of the system and let F(t) be the cumulative distribution function of T, then the reliability is given by

$$R(t) = 1 - F(t), \ t \geq 0.$$

The *failure rate* (or hazard rate, force of mortality, failure intensity), r(t), of F(t) is defined as

$$r(t) = \underset{\Delta t \to 0}{Lim} \frac{R(t) - R(\Delta t + t)}{\Delta t R(t)} = \frac{f(t)}{R(t)}.$$

In the above f(t) which is the derivative of F(t) is called the density function of F(t). Note that r(t)Δt may be interpreted as the conditional probability of failure in [t,t+Δt) given that a system has survived up to time t.

Other equivalent relations are

$$r(t) = \frac{f(t)}{1 - F(t)} = \frac{d}{dt}[-ln(1 - F(t))] = \frac{d}{dt}[-lnR(t)].$$

It should be noted here that similar definitions are applicable for repairable systems although the terminologies are sometimes confusing. We will use the term failure intensity when talking about the instantaneous failure occurrence rate of a repairable process and failure rate for a random quantity according to the definition above. Sometimes r(t) is called ROCOF (Rate Of oCcurrence Of Failure) when talking about repairable systems.

The failure rate function is interesting from a reliability point of view since it is strongly connected with aging properties of life distributions. Many classes of life distributions have been defined and studied based on the shape of this failure rate function, such as IFR- (increasing failure rate) distributions and DFR- (decreasing failure rate) distributions. Interested readers are referred to standard literature of reliability theory listed at the end of this chapter.

The density function f(t), the cumulative distribution function F(t), the reliability function R(t) and the failure rate function r(t) are all closely related to each other. Under very general conditions, any of them uniquely determines the other three.

Given the failure rate function r(t), the reliability function R(t) may be calculated by

$$R(t) = exp\left\{-\int_0^t r(s)\,ds\right\}.$$

Also, given the failure rate function r(t), the density function f(t) may be determined by

$$f(t) = r(t)\,exp\left\{-\int_0^t r(s)\,ds\right\}.$$

The most important characteristic measure of reliability is the expectation of the time to failure, defined as

$$ET = \int_0^\infty tf(t)\,dt = \int_0^\infty R(t)\,dt.$$

Given the reliability function, this is thus a measure of the average time to failure for a component with life distribution F(t).

2.4.2. Some useful distributions in reliability engineering

The most widely used distribution function in reliability analysis is the exponential distribution. Due to many of its useful properties, exponential distribution has become the most commonly applied life distribution. The *exponential distribution* with parameter α, simply denoted by *Exp(α)*, has density function

$$f(t) = \alpha^{-1}e^{-t/\alpha}.$$

The corresponding distribution function is simply given by

$$F(t) = 1 - e^{-t/\alpha}.$$

The failure rate function of an exponential distribution with parameter α is a constant which equals to

$$r(t) = \lambda = \frac{1}{\alpha}.$$

A random variable T having exponential distribution function will be called exponential. Both the mean and the standard deviation of an exponentially distributed random variable with parameter α are equal to α.

The most important characteristic of exponential distribution is its memoryless property. The conditional distribution of survival t+s time units given that it has survived s time units is the same as the probability of surviving t time units for a new component, that is

$$P(T>t+s|T>s) = P(T>t), for\ all\ t,s>0.$$

It should be noted that memoryless property, constant-failure rate property and exponentiality are equivalent conditions of a nonnegative random variable. The constancy of the failure rate function is very interesting and unique. Any unit with exponential distributed life time has no aging. Since this is usually the case for software, exponential distribution is very important in studying software reliability.

A direct generalization of the exponential distribution is the *Weibull distribution*. The density function of the Weibull distribution with parameter α and β, *Weibull(α, β)*, is

$$f(t) = \beta \alpha^{-\beta} t^{\beta-1} exp\left\{-\left(\frac{t}{\alpha}\right)^{\beta}\right\}.$$

The distribution function of the Weibull(α,β) is simply given by

$$F(t) = 1 - exp\left\{-\left(\frac{t}{\alpha}\right)^{\beta}\right\},\ \alpha>0,\ \beta>0,$$

and α is called the scale parameter and β is the shape parameter. The corresponding failure rate function is

$$r(t) = \beta \alpha^{-\beta} t^{\beta-1}.$$

It can be easily seen that for a Weibull distribution r(t) is increasing for $\beta > 1$ and decreasing for $\beta < 1$. This flexibility is very important in studying reliability of many mechanical systems. However, for software systems, we may expect that $\beta = 1$ which is exponential distribution with no aging.

The density function of the *Gamma distribution* with scale parameter α and shape parameter β, *Gamma(α, β)*, is

$$f(t) = \frac{t^{\beta-1}}{\alpha^{\beta} \Gamma(\beta)} e^{-t/\alpha}, \quad \alpha > 0, \beta > 0,$$

where $\Gamma(\beta)$ is the so called *Gamma function* defined as

$$\Gamma(\beta) = \int_0^{\infty} x^{\beta-1} e^{-x} dx.$$

For integer β, we have that by integrating f(t),

$$F(t) = 1 - e^{-t/\alpha} \sum_{k=0}^{\beta-1} \frac{(t/\alpha)^k}{k!}.$$

The Gamma distribution can be obtained from sums of independent, identically distributed exponential random variables. It can be shown that if $T_1, T_2, ..., T_n$ are exponentially distributed random variables with the same parameter α, then

$$T = T_1 + T_2 + ... + T_n$$

is Gamma(α,n).

Both the Weibull distribution and the Gamma distribution are generalizations of the exponential distribution. Both reduce to the exponential distribution with parameter $\beta=1$. A Weibull distribution with $\beta=2$ is also called *Rayleigh distribution*. A Gamma distribution with scale parameter $\alpha=2$ and shape parameter $\beta=2n$ is called χ^2 distribution with n degrees of freedom.

The most useful distribution in statistics is the so called *normal distribution* (or Gauss distribution). The normal distribution with mean μ and standard variation σ, $N(\mu,\sigma)$, has distribution function

$$F(t) = \Phi\left(\frac{t-\mu}{\sigma}\right),$$

where $\Phi(t)$ is the standard normal distribution function defined as

$$\Phi(t) = \frac{1}{\sqrt{2\pi}} \int_{-\infty}^{t} exp\left\{-\frac{x^2}{2}\right\} dx.$$

Hence, the density function of a normally distributed random variable with parameter μ and σ is given by

$$f(t) = \frac{1}{\sigma\sqrt{2\pi}} exp\left\{-\frac{1}{2}\left(\frac{t-\mu}{\sigma}\right)^2\right\}.$$

Sometimes a random variable X is of a discrete nature, for example the number of software faults, which may be treated as a random quantity. Such random variables take values on a discrete space and some important discrete distributions are the following.

The *Poisson distribution* with parameter μ is given by

$$P(X=k) = \frac{\mu^k e^{-\mu}}{k!}, \quad k \geq 0;$$

and it is a widely used distribution for the number of events within some observed time. It has also many desirable properties, e.g. the expectation of a Poisson distribution is equal to μ. A general class of stochastic processes called Poisson process is also closely related to Poisson distribution.

The *binomial distribution* with parameters (n,p) is given by

$$P(X=k) = \binom{n}{k} p^k (1-p)^{n-k}, \quad k=0,1,\dots,n.$$

The mean of a binomial distribution is equal to np. Binomial distribution arises for example when we consider the total number of events in Bernoulli trials. Poisson distribution may also be considered as the limiting case of binomial distribution by letting $n\to\infty$, $p\to0$ together with the condition $np\to\mu$.

The *geometric distribution* with parameter p is given by

$$P(X=k) = (1-p)p^k, \quad k\geq0.$$

The geometric distribution is the discrete counterpart of the exponential distribution. It has also a memoryless property in a discrete sense. The mean of a random quantity having geometric distribution is 1/p.

The *hypergeometric distribution* has a distribution function

$$P(X=k) = \frac{\binom{M}{k}\binom{N-M}{n-k}}{\binom{N}{n}}, \quad 0\leq k\leq n\leq N \text{ and } k\leq M,$$

where n, N and M are parameters. The expectation of this distribution is equal to nM/N.

2.4.3. Estimation of parameters

Usually, parameters in software reliability models are not known and they have to be estimated by using collected failure data. There are many estimation methods which can be used for the purpose of statistical inference. The most common one is the method of maximum likelihood. Here, we briefly describe this method because of its extensive use in software reliability literature. For other methods, such as the method of least squares and the method of moments which are also used in practice we refer the readers to other standard statistical literature. The Bayesian estimation will be discussed in a separate chapter, Chapter 6, later in this book.

Let T_1, T_2, ..., T_n be a random sample of size n drawn from a probability density function $f_i(t_i, \theta)$, i=1,2,...,n, where θ is an unknown parameter. Then the likelihood function of the parameter θ for this random sample is the joint density of these n random variables, that is

$$L(\theta|t_1, t_2, \dots, t_n) = \prod_{i=1}^{n} f_i(t_i, \theta).$$

The value of θ which maximizes the likelihood function $L(\theta|t_1, t_2, ..., t_n)$, is called the maximum likelihood estimator of θ. Usually the maximization of the likelihood function has to be carried out by using some appropriate numerical methods. In practice, the following procedure can lead to some simplification.

By taking the natural logarithm of $L(\theta|t_1, t_2, ..., t_n)$ and then the derivative with respect to θ, and letting it be equal to zero, we get the so-called likelihood equation for solving θ, that is

$$\frac{\partial}{\partial \theta} lnL(\theta|t_1, t_2, \dots, t_n) = 0.$$

By inserting the expression of $L(\theta|t_1, t_2, ..., t_n)$, we simply get

$$\frac{\partial}{\partial \theta} lnL(\theta|t_1, t_2, \dots, t_n) = \frac{\partial}{\partial \theta} ln\prod_{i=1}^{n} f_i(t_i, \theta)$$

$$= \frac{\partial}{\partial \theta} \sum_{i=1}^{n} lnf_i(t_i, \theta) = \sum_{i=1}^{n} \frac{\partial}{\partial \theta} lnf_i(t_i, \theta) = 0.$$

The maximum likelihood estimate has several very desirable properties. It is, under certain general conditions, an asymptotically normal and efficient estimate of θ. It is also invariant, that is, if $\hat{\theta}$ is the maximum likelihood estimate for θ and $a(\theta)$ is a function of θ, then $a(\hat{\theta})$ is the maximum likelihood estimate for $a(\theta)$.

The above procedure can easily be generalized to multi-dimensional cases when we have a vector of parameters. Details and other statistical estimation techniques may be found in most of the elementary texts on statistics, such as those in the bibliographic notes in the following.

2.5. Bibliographic notes

There are many general papers discussing the software reliability concepts and problems encountered in this chapter. For general introductory papers interested readers are referred to the papers in the bibliographic notes of the previous chapter.

Some of the recent books presenting the probabilistic and statistic approaches of reliability analysis are:

Barlow, R.E. and Proschan, F. (1981). *Reliability Theory and Life Testing*. To Begin With, New York.

Gertsbakh, I.B. (1989). *Statistical Reliability Theory*. Marcel Dekker, New York.

Lawless, J.W. (1982). *Statistical Models and Methods for Lifetime Data*. Wiley, New York.

Ross, S.M. (1983). *Introduction to Probability Models*. Academic Press, New York.

Smith, D.J. (1985). *Reliability and Maintainability in Perspective*. MacMillan Publishers Ltd., London.

Tobias, P.A. and Trindade, D.C. (1986). *Applied Reliability*. Van Norstrand Reinhold, New York.

3

Markov Models

In this chapter we present some existing software reliability models for which a Markov assumption is made. For this type of models the software failure process is described by a Markov process. The Markov assumption implies the memoryless property of the process which is a helpful simplification of many stochastic models and it is associated with the exponentiality. The exponential distribution has many interesting properties and its simplicity has made it the most widely used distribution in reliability analysis. First some general introductions to Markov process modelling is presented. Then the Jelinski-Moranda model which is one of the earliest software reliability models is discussed. Historically, this model has had a very strong influence on many later software reliability models and it is often referred to. Generalizations and modifications of this model are studied in later sections. At the end of this chapter, we have also included some existing Markov reliability models useful in a system context, such as Markov models of modular software and Markov availability models. Finally, a bibliographic note ends this chapter.

3.1. General theory of Markov process modelling

Markov processes which are a general class of stochastic processes have been widely used and studied in reliability analyses. Many software reliability models also belong to this category. A Markov process is characterized by its state space together with the transition probabilities between these states.

A stochastic process $\{X(t), t \geq 0\}$ is said to be a Markov process if its future development depends only on the present state of the process, that is

$$P[X(t) \geq x(t) | X(t_1) \geq x_1, \ldots, X(t_n) \geq x_n] = P[X(t) \geq x(t) | X(t_n) \geq x_n],$$

for all $t_1 < t_2 < \ldots < t_n < t$.

The above property is generally called the Markov property which has the following simple explanation. Given the present state of the process, its future behaviour is independent of the past history of the process. This is the most important characteristic of a Markov process and although this needs not always be the case, it is a realistic simplification in many practical situations.

If the state space is discrete, a Markov process is also called the Markov chain. Define p_{ij} is the transition probability of the process between state i and state j, that is

$$p_{ij}(t+s) = P[X(t+s)=j \,|\, X(s)=i], \; s,t>0.$$

In general p_{ij} may depend on t as well as on s. If all p_{ij}, i,j>0, are independent of t, the Markov chain is called time-homogeneous.

The most famous result of a homogeneous continuous-time Markov chain is that it satisfies the so-called Kolmogorov equations, that is

$$p_{ij}(t+s) = \sum_k p_{ik}(s)p_{kj}(t), \; s,t>0.$$

The theory of Markov processes is well developed. The initial condition of the process together with the transition probabilities completely determines the stochastic behaviour of the Markov process. Knowing the transition probabilities, the probability that the process is in a certain state can be obtained by solving the Kolmogorov equations, and other reliability measures can also be calculated. However, in order to get a mathematically tractable software reliability model, some further assumptions usually have to be made.

Generally, each sojourn time interval for a Markov process, i.e. the time between two events, has an exponential distribution with the parameter dependent on the state being visited. Another property is that times between transitions are conditionally independent of each other given the successive states being visited. These properties together with the fact that the successive states visited form a Markov chain clarify the structure of a Markov process.

Other standard results can be found in many elementary texts on stochastic processes. Also in many books on reliability Markov process models are discussed.

The process {N(t), t≥0} where N(t) is the number of events in a Markov process, such as the number of detected faults in a software context, is called a Markov counting process. In software reliability analysis an important class of Markov process is the birth-death process for which a so-called birth increases the size of the process by one and a death decreases the size by one.

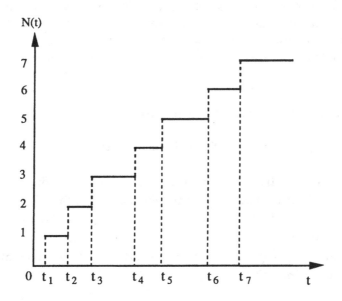

Figure 3.1. A realization of a Markov counting process {N(t),t≥0}.

Markov models are very useful in studying software fault-removal processes, especially, they are useful during the software testing phase which is the most important one of software development. It is in this phase that software faults are detected and removed. The state of the process at time t is here the number of remaining faults at that time.

The fault-removal process can usually be described by a so-called pure death process since the number of remaining faults is a decreasing function of time provided that no new faults are introduced. If we also consider the introduction of new faults due to incorrect debugging, the so-called birth-death processes can then be used in studying software reliability during the testing phase.

3.2. The Jelinski-Moranda (JM) model

The best-known software reliability model originally developed by Jelinski and Moranda (1972) is also a Markov process model. It is one of the earliest models and has strongly influenced many later models which are in fact modifications of this simple model. In this section we present the JM-model in detail and further generalizations of this model will be discussed in later sections.

3.2.1. Model assumptions and some properties

The underlying assumptions of the JM-model are:

(1) the number of initial software faults is an unknown but fixed constant;
(2) a detected fault is removed immediately and no new fault is introduced;
(3) times between failures are independent, exponentially distributed random quantities;
(4) all remaining software faults contribute the same amount to the software failure intensity.

Denote by N_0 the number of software faults in the software before the testing starts. By the assumption (3) and (4), the initial failure intensity is then equal to $N_0\phi$, where ϕ is a constant of proportionality denoting the failure intensity contributed by each fault. It follows from assumption (2) that, after a new fault is detected and removed, the number of remaining faults is decreased by one. Hence after the k:th failure, there are (N_0-k) faults left, and the failure intensity decreases to $\phi(N_0-k)$.

Denote by T_i, $i=1,2,...,N_0$, the time between the (i-1):th and the i:th failures, T_i is thus the i:th failure-free time interval. By the assumptions, T_i's are then exponentially distributed random variables with parameter

$$\lambda(i) = \phi[N_0 - (i-1)], \quad i=1,2,\ldots,N_0.$$

The distribution of T_i is given by

$$P(T_i < t_i) = \phi(N_0-i+1)exp\{-\phi(N_0-i+1)t_i\}, \quad i=1,2,\ldots,N_0.$$

The main property of the JM-model is that the failure intensity is constant between the detection of two consecutive failures. This is quite reasonable if the software is unchanged and the testing is random and homogeneous. A plot of the failure intensity function versus the cumulative time is displayed in Figure 3.2. In Figure 3.3 a plot of $\lambda(i)$ versus the number of detected faults i can also be found.

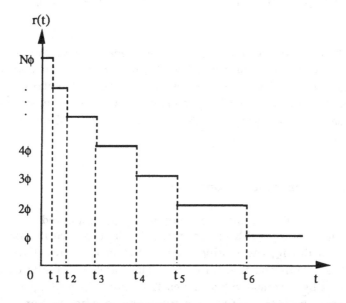

Figure 3.2. A realization of failure intensity as a function of time. For each removal of a fault, the failure intensity decreases by ϕ.

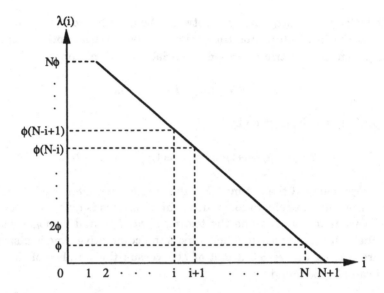

Figure 3.3. The failure intensity versus the number of removed faults.

It should be pointed out here that this simple model has an order statistic explanation. Successive failure times constitute order statistics of N_0 independent random variables from an exponential distribution with parameter ϕ. General order statistic models have been studied by various authors, see e.g. Langberg and Singpurwalla (1985), Miller (1986) and Mellor (1987).

3.2.2. Estimation of model parameters

The parameters of the JM-model may easily be estimated by using the method of maximum likelihood. Let t_i denote the observed i:th failure-free time interval during the testing phase, that is t_i is the observed time between the (i-1):th and the i:th failure. The number of faults detected is denoted here by n which will be called the sample size. Suppose that the failure data set $\tilde{t}=\{t_1,t_2,...,t_n; n>0\}$, is given, the parameters ϕ and N_0 in the JM-model can easily be estimated by maximizing the likelihood function.

The likelihood function of the parameters N_0 and ϕ is given by

$$L(t_1, t_2, \ldots, t_n; N_0, \phi) = \prod_{i=1}^{n} \phi(N_0 - i + 1) exp\left\{-\phi(N_0 - i + 1)t_i\right\}$$

$$= \phi^n \left\{\prod_{i=1}^{n} (N_0 - i + 1)\right\} exp\left\{-\phi \sum_{i=1}^{n} (N_0 - i + 1)t_i\right\}.$$

The natural logarithm of the above likelihood function is

$$lnL = ln\left[\phi^n \left\{\prod_{i=1}^{n} (N_0 - i + 1)\right\} exp\left\{-\phi \sum_{i=1}^{n} (N_0 - i + 1)t_i\right\}\right]$$

$$= ln\phi^n + ln\left\{\prod_{i=1}^{n} (N_0 - i + 1)\right\} - \phi \sum_{i=1}^{n} (N_0 - i + 1)t_i$$

$$= n\,ln\phi + \sum_{i=1}^{n} ln(N_0 - i + 1) - \phi \sum_{i=1}^{n} (N_0 - i + 1)t_i.$$

By taking the partial derivatives of this log-likelihood function with respect to N_0 and ϕ, respectively, and equating them to zero, we get the following likelihood equations

$$\frac{\partial lnL}{\partial N_0} = \sum_{i=1}^{n} \frac{1}{N_0 - i + 1} - \sum_{i=1}^{n} \phi t_i = 0,$$

$$\frac{\partial lnL}{\partial \phi} = \frac{n}{\phi} - \sum_{i=1}^{n} (N_0 - i + 1)t_i = 0.$$

Usually numerical procedures have to be used to solve these two equations. However, the equation system can be simplified as follows. By solving ϕ from the second equation above we get

$$\phi = n\left\{\sum_{i=1}^{n} (N_0 - i + 1)t_i\right\}^{-1},$$

and by inserting this into the first equation, we obtain an equation independent of ϕ,

$$\frac{1}{N_0} + \frac{1}{N_0-1} + \ldots + \frac{1}{N_0-n+1} = \frac{n \, \Sigma_{i=1}^{n} t_i}{\Sigma_{i=1}^{n}(N_0-i+1)t_i}.$$

The estimate of N_0 can then be obtained by solving this equation. Inserting the estimated N_0 into the expression of ϕ, we may then get the maximum likelihood estimate of ϕ.

3.2.3. Notes on the maximum likelihood estimates

A brief discussion about the maximum likelihood estimates of the parameters is in its place here. Maximum likelihood estimation of the parameters in the JM-model has been widely studied and many authors have also reported problems associated with this method. Especially for the estimation of the number of initial faults we usually get unreasonable results, see e.g. Forman and Singpurwalla (1977) and (1979), Littlewood (1981b) and Joe and Reid (1985a).

Although the estimation using the method of maximum likelihood is straightforward and the asymptotic behaviour of the estimates can easily be determined using the large sample theory of maximum likelihood estimators, there are many problems here. The maximum likelihood estimate of the number of initial faults may not exist for some data sets and when it exists, it often gives unreasonable results, such as nearly infinite number of faults, or no further faults remaining. Another problem is its instability that makes us unable to trust the results.

However, The problem is not at all surprising, if we consider it from a statistical point of view. The probability of getting disordered data such as observing more failures when there probably should be less, is quite high because failure processes are random processes. If this occurs, it will lead to infinite estimate of the number of initial faults with large probability and this makes the maximum likelihood estimator unsatisfactory as a point estimator, see Joe and Reid (1985a).

Generally, under the assumptions of the JM-model, the likelihood function has a unique maximum at a finite N_0 and a positive ϕ if, and only if, the following inequality is satisfied, see e.g. Littlewood and Verrall (1981),

$$\frac{\sum_{i=1}^{n}(i-1)t_i}{\sum_{i=1}^{n}(i-1)} > \frac{\sum_{i=1}^{n}t_i}{n}.$$

The above inequality can be shown to be equivalent to

$$\frac{\sum_{i=1}^{n}(i-1)t_i}{\sum_{i=1}^{n}t_i} > \frac{1}{2(n-1)}.$$

The estimation problem has also been discussed in Speij (1985) which shows that if the above inequality is reversed, the likelihood function is an increasing function of N and hence we have an infinite estimate of the number of software faults. Some more general results may also be found in Wright and Hazelhurst (1988) and Huang (1990).

The solution of these problems can be the following. Firstly, the number of faults is not a characteristic measure of software reliability because faults do not have the same size and having many faults is not the same as having a low reliability. In fact, the software is likely so, at a later stage of the testing phase, that it still contains many faults but each with very low detection probability. This may explain the fact that the JM-model usually underestimates the number of remaining faults. Because the number of faults and the average size of fault is, in a sense, indistinguishable, we should try to estimate the reliability function or the current failure intensity instead of the number of remaining faults. It has been observed that the estimate of the current failure intensity is usually reasonable and decreases are relatively stable, as the number of faults removed increases, see e.g. Xie and Åkerlund (1989).

Secondly, Bayesian inference or Bayesian models are very helpful in utilizing information to make more accurate estimation. The experiences gained during the development of the software should be utilized. Also, we usually do have failure data from similar software systems developed previously which may provide us with useful information that should be used. Bayesian extension of the JM-model has been studied by many authors and in Section 6.3 some existing Bayesian formulations of the JM-model are presented.

Thirdly, in many cases the JM-model is not necessarily good and this leads us to searching for more realistic models. The assumption that all software faults contribute the same amount to the failure intensity is certainly unrealistic. It is reasonable to assume that some faults are much easier to be detected than others. Hence, models which are able to incorporate this are desirable. In the following section we will present a more general formulation and provide some similar models obtained under some simple modifications of these assumptions.

3.3. Decreasing Failure Intensity (DFI) models

A serious critique of the JM-model is that not all software faults are of the same size. Some faults are more easily detected than others. By incorporating this fact, some generalizations and modifications of the JM-model are presented in Xie (1987). We briefly describe this general formulation together with some special cases in this section. Some heuristic arguments leading to specific models are also presented.

3.3.1. A general DFI formulation

The JM-model can be modified by using other jump intensity function $\lambda(i)$. Note that $\lambda(i)$ is defined as the rate of the occurrence of the next failure after the removal of the (i-1):th fault. We say that a failure intensity function $\lambda(i)$ is DFI (Decreasing Failure Intensity) if $\lambda(i)$ is a decreasing function of i. A DFI model is thus a Markov counting process model with decreasing failure intensity function.

The general assumptions of the DFI Markov model are the same as those for the JM-model. The failure counting process is assumed to be a Markov counting process. We also assume that all detected faults are immediately removed and no new faults are introduced during the testing. It should be noted here that these assumptions have lower order effects on software reliability and failure data can usually be modified in practice by e.g. counting the number of detected faults instead of the number of failures, if a fault has caused more than one failures. Also, we assume here that the test is completely random, that is, test data are taken randomly from the input space of the software. Under the Markov assumption, the times between failures are exponentially distributed with parameter $\lambda(i)$.

Since software failure process is a reliability growth process, by detecting and removing software faults, the reliability does increase. The failure intensity between the removals of two faults should also be constant, provided that the testing is random and homogeneous and if the software is not subjected to any change. However, the shape of the failure intensity as a function of the number of removed faults may take different forms, depending on the inherent nature of the software.

It can be observed that the failure intensity function $\lambda(i)$ for the JM-model is a linear function of the number of remaining faults. In fact, since at the beginning big faults are likely to be detected, the decrease of the failure intensity is probably larger at the beginning than that at the end of the testing phase. As a function of the number of remaining faults, the failure intensity function is likely to be a convex function. Note that if all software faults are removed, then the software will never fail. Hence, if a model for finite number of faults will be used, another general requirement on $\lambda(i)$ is that $\lambda(N_0+1)=0$, that is, the failure intensity should be zero when the last fault has been removed.

Under the general assumptions above, the cumulative number of faults detected and removed, $\{N(t), t \geq 0\}$, is a Markov counting process with decreasing failure intensity $\lambda(i)$. The theory for continuous time Markov chains can be applied. It can be shown that the collection of probabilities

$$\{p_i(t) = P[N(t)=i]; \ i=0,1,2,...,N_0, \ t \geq 0\}$$

satisfies the so-called Kolmogorov's differential equations. The forward form of these equations are given as follows

$$p_0'(t) = -\lambda(1)p_0(t),$$

$$p_1'(t) = -\lambda(2)p_1(t) + \lambda(1)p_0(t),$$

$$\cdot$$
$$\cdot$$
$$\cdot$$

$$p_i'(t) = -\lambda(i+1)p_i(t) + \lambda(i)p_{i-1}(t), \quad i<N_0,$$

and

$$p_{N_0}'(t) = \lambda(N_0)p_{N_0-1}(t).$$

Furthermore, the assumption $N(0)=0$ yields the following initial conditions

$$p_0(0)=1 \; and \; p_i(0)=0 \; for \; i>0.$$

The above Kolmogorov's differential equations can easily be solved and the solution is as follows

$$p_0(t) = e^{-\lambda(1)t},$$

$$p_1(t) = \frac{\lambda(1)}{\lambda(2) - \lambda(1)}(e_1 - e_0),$$

$$\vdots$$

$$p_i(t) = \sum_{j=0}^{i} A_j^{(i)}e_j, \quad i<N_0;$$

and for $i=N_0$, we have,

$$p_{N_0}(t) = -\sum_{j=0}^{N_0-1} A_j^{(N_0-1)}\frac{\lambda(N_0)}{\lambda(j+1)}e_j,$$

where the quantities e_j, $j=0,1,...,$ N_0-1, are defined as

$$e_j = e^{-\lambda(j+1)t}, \quad j=0,1,2,...,N_0-1.$$

The quantities $A_j^{(i)}$ can be calculated recursively through

$$A_j^{(i)} = \frac{\lambda(i)}{\lambda(i+1) - \lambda(j+1)} A_j^{(i-1)}, \quad j<i;$$

and

$$A_i^{(i)} = -\sum_{j=0}^{i-1} A_j^{(i)}.$$

Generally, for a DFI model with parameter $\lambda(i)$, we have a set of parameters to be determined by using collected failure data. The estimation of the parameters can be carried out by using the method of maximum likelihood. The likelihood function of the $\lambda(i)$ is given by

$$L(n,\lambda(\cdot)) = \prod_{i=1}^{n} \lambda(i) \exp\{-\lambda(i)t_i\}.$$

The parameters in $\lambda(i)$ can thus be estimated by maximizing this likelihood function. Usually, numerical methods must be used, see e.g. Xie and Bergman (1988) for some procedures and numerical results.

3.3.2. Some specific DFI models

As discussed previously, software faults are not likely of the same size which is also the most serious drawback of the JM-model. It is reasonable to assume that earlier failures are caused by faults having a high detection probability. A direct generalization of the JM-model is to use a power-type function for $\lambda(i)$.

The power type DFI Markov model studied in Xie and Bergman (1988) assumes that the failure intensity $\lambda(i)$ is a power-type function of the number of remaining faults, that is

$$\lambda(i) = \phi[N_0 - (i-1)]^{\alpha}, \ i=1,2,\ldots,N_0.$$

Due to the reasons discussed previously, $\lambda(i)$ should decrease fast at the beginning and the decrease becomes slower for each i. Hence, it is reasonable to assume that $\lambda(i)$ is a convex function of i and α is likely to be greater than one, since in this case, the decrease of the failure intensity is larger at the beginning, see Figure 3.4.

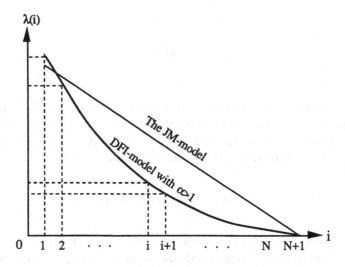

Figure 3.4. The power-type failure intensity function
versus the number of detected faults.

The exponential-type Markov DFI model assumes that the failure intensity
is an exponential function of the number of remaining faults. It is
characterized by the failure intensity function

$$\lambda(i) = \phi\left[e^{-\beta(N_0 - i + 1)} - 1\right], \ i = 1, 2, \dots, N_0.$$

For the exponential-type DFI model, the decrease of the failure intensity at
the beginning is much faster than that at a later phase.

In the following sections we will give some heuristic motivations of the
reality of these models using a size-biased sampling argument. Under
some reasonable conditions, we may derive the above two models under the
assumption that each fault is detected with a probability proportional to its
size which is here defined as the number of input data which will lead to a
failure due to the fault. Hence, larger faults are in this case detected earlier
and this removes the most unrealistic assumption involved in the JM-
model.

The following observations can be noted. The power-type DFI model is a direct generalization of the JM-model which corresponds to the case $\alpha=1$. The parameter α can be treated as a new parameter and in this case, we have a three-parametric model. It is possible to reduce it to a two-parametric model by using a fixed value of α. For example, a reasonable value for α is two, as shown by the heuristic arguments in the following sections.

It is interesting to note that the exponential-type DFI model is similar to that of the Geometric De-Eutrophication model suggested by Moranda (1975). Usually, a software can never be completely fault-free and we may assume that there are an infinite number of faults in the software and the detection rate per fault ϕ is infinitely small. These assumptions together with the condition

$$\phi b^{N_0+1} \to a,$$

where a and b are unknown constants, gives

$$\lambda(i) = ab^{i-1};\ i \geq 1.$$

This is just the failure intensity after removing i faults for the Moranda Geometric De-Eutrophication model, see the paper by Moranda (1975) where the original idea is to derive a model for the case when we have an infinite number of faults.

A similar model has been studied by Currit et al. (1986) where the mean time to next failure after m changes of the software is estimated by

$$MTTF_m = MTTF_0 R^m,$$

where $MTTF_m$ is the mean time to failure after m changes. In the above R and m are other model parameters.

3.3.3. Validation of the exponentiality

The power-type and exponential-type DFI model can be derived by using a heuristic size-biased sampling argument. Usually, a large fault corresponds to a large failure probability and this implies that larger faults are likely to be detected earlier than smaller faults are. The assumption that all faults have the same size is the most critical one for the JM-model and it is this assumption that we try to eliminate.

The argument consists of two stages. In this section, we prove that under the random testing assumption, the failure times are exponentially distributed, which implies that the failure process has a memoryless property. If we define the size of a fault as the number of input data which may give incorrect output due to this fault, then a larger fault contributes more to the total failure intensity than a smaller one does. We then, in the next section, show that if each fault has a geometrically distributed size, then the power-type DFI function with $\alpha=2$ seems to be appropriate. Note that the geometric distribution is a discrete counterpart of the exponential distribution which is a reasonable assumption, see e.g. Bishop et al. (1987).

Let M be the size of the input data space, i.e. the number of data which can be used as input to the software. The quantity M is assumed to be very large but finite for the sake of simplicity. One reason that M cannot be infinite in practice is that all data which can be stored in a computer are truncated and the number of data is limited. Note that an input datum can be multi-dimensional. Let M^* be the total number of these input data which may cause software failure. We also assume that M^* is much smaller than M since otherwise the software system is too bad to be analysed statistically.

Suppose that input data arrive at the software system according to a Poisson process with intensity function ω which can be interpreted as the intensity of testing. Then the probability that the software encounters no failure in a time interval of length t is

$$1 - F(t) = \sum_{j=0}^{\infty} \left(\frac{e^{-\omega t}(\omega t)^j}{j!} \right) \left(\frac{M - M^*}{M} \right)^j,$$

given M, M^* and ω.

Note that this has a shock model interpretation, see e.g. Langberg and Singpurwalla (1985). The first term inside the summation sign denotes the probability that j inputs or shocks are received during the time interval [0,t) while the second term inside the summation sign denotes the probability that none of the j inputs causes any failure of the software.

If we let λ be a quantity defined as

$$\lambda = \frac{M^*}{M}\omega,$$

then it is easy to verify that

$$\sum_{j=0}^{\infty}\left(\frac{e^{-\omega t}(\omega t)^j}{j!}\right)\left(\frac{M-M^*}{M}\right)^j = e^{-\lambda t},$$

and we have that the time to next failure has the following distribution

$$F(t) = 1 - e^{-\lambda t},$$

which implies that, if λ does not depend on t, then the time to next failure of the software is exponentially distributed with parameter λ.

The above shock model interpretation of software testing remains valid, even in the case when all parameters depend on the number of removed software faults which usually is the case. Generally, we have that T_i, the time between the (i-1):th and the i:th failure of the software, has a distribution function,

$$F(t) = P(T_i \leq t) = 1 - e^{-\lambda(i)t},$$

It should be pointed out here that usually $\lambda(i)$ may also be a function of time. If this is the case, the exponentiality assumption is not valid and we have to use other distributions. However, if the system is specified and it does not suffer from any great change, then this time dependence should be very weak, provided also that the test is homogeneous in the sense that the test intensity is constant on a reasonable scale, such as calendar time, man-power time or CPU-time whichever is suitable. Hence, we may assume that $\lambda(i)$ is not time-dependent and we really have exponentially distributed times between failures.

3.3.4. Heuristic arguments of some special cases

Following the above section, we derive here some specific models under some appropriate conditions. The derivation is based on heuristic size-biased sampling arguments. First we study a simple case which leads to the JM-model and then some modifications are made by using more realistic assumptions.

Let $M_k>0$ be the number of input data which may lead to a software failure due to the k:th fault. Then, after removing the i:th fault, the number of input data which may cause any failure is given by

$$M^*(i) = \sum_{j=i+1}^{N_0} M_j,$$

assuming that all faults cause disjoint sets of input data to fail. In the above N_0 denotes the total number of initial faults in the software.

Suppose that the input space of the software does not depend on i and note that M^* is a decreasing function of i which is a consequence from the above formula since M_j are all positive quantities. If the test intensity function ω is a constant, independent of time, then times between failures are exponentially distributed with a parameter which decreases as a function of i, as noted in the previous section. This is the same model as the general Markov process model with decreasing failure intensity.

Assume that all faults in the software have the same size, i.e. $M_k=M_0$, for all $k=1,2,...,N_0$. This means that the number of the input data which cause a failure is reduced by the same size M_0, independent of which fault is removed next, see e.g. Figure 3.5. Assume further that all faults are independent of each other. Then it is easily seen that the time between the (i-1):th and the i:th failure, T_i, is exponentially distributed with parameter $\phi(N_0-i+1)$ which is the same as that for the JM-model. Hence, the JM-model is a very special case of the general derivation described above.

As pointed out before, one of the most unreasonable assumptions made for the JM-model and many other existing models is that all faults in the software have the same size. Other assumptions such as the correct and immediate removal of any detected fault are less critical and failure data can be modified by counting the time of the detection of an initial fault. In the following, we will use a size-biased sampling reasoning in the derivation of some other DFI models.

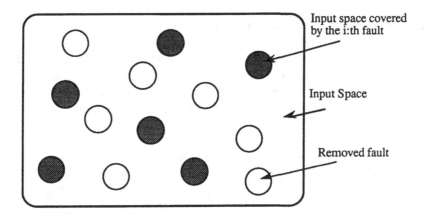

Figure 3.5. For the JM-model all faults are of the same size.

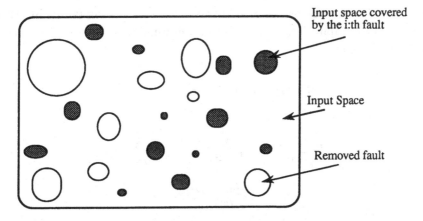

Figure 3.6. Generally, faults are not of equal size and large faults are likely to be detected at the beginning.

After detecting the i:th fault, there are (N_0-i) undetected faults left in the software. The average size of these remaining faults, $\overline{M}_i$, is then

$$\overline{M}_i = \frac{M^*(i)}{N_0 - i} = \frac{1}{N_0 - i} \sum_{j=i+1}^{N_0} M_j .$$

Since usually, M_j's are unknown and can be treated as random quantities, we may adapt some sampling arguments here. Usually, a fault with a large M_j is likely to be chosen at the beginning and this is the case when we have a sampling proportional to size which is also called size-biased sampling. Because M_j's are not of the same size, a randomly chosen one has a size which usually is larger than the average size, see e.g. Figure 3.6.

Now we assume that M_i is twice as large as the average which is denoted by $\overline{M}_i$. This can be justified if M_k has a size which is geometrically distributed. Using a size-biased sampling argument it follows that the i:th removed fault is, in this case, about twice as large as the average size of the remaining faults. Note that this is similar to a renewal theoretical argument which states that in a Poisson process the expected length of a randomly chosen interval is exactly twice the average length.

If M_i is twice as large as the average size of the remaining faults, $\overline{M}_i$, then the number of input data which cause a failure after removing the (i+1):th fault, $M^*(i+1)$, is

$$M^*(i+1) = M^*(i) - M_{i+1} = \sum_{j=i+1}^{N_0} M_j - 2\overline{M}_i$$

$$= \sum_{j=i+1}^{N_0} M_j - \frac{2}{N_0 - i} \sum_{j=i+1}^{N_0} M_j = \frac{N_0 - i - 2}{N_0 - i} \sum_{j=i+1}^{N_0} M_j$$

$$= \frac{N_0 - i - 2}{N_0 - i} M^*(i).$$

Hence, it follows that the failure intensity after removing the (i+1):th fault can be calculated as follows,

$$\lambda(i+1) = \frac{\omega}{M} M^*(i+1)$$

$$= \frac{N_0-i+-2}{N_0-i} \cdot \frac{\omega}{M} M^*(i) = \frac{N_0-i-2}{N_0-i} \lambda(i)$$

$$= \frac{N_0-i-2}{N_0-i} \cdot \frac{N_0-i-1}{N_0-i+1} \cdot \ \ldots \ \cdot \frac{N_0-3}{N_0-1} \cdot \frac{N_0-2}{N_0} \lambda(0)$$

$$= (N_0-i-2)(N_0-i-1)\frac{\lambda(0)}{(N_0-1)N_0}$$

where $\lambda(0)$ is a constant. If we assume that N_0 is large, then we have

$$\lambda(i+1) \approx (N_0-i)^2\lambda_0 \propto (N_0-i)^2.$$

It follows now that the failure intensity decreases quadratically as the number of remaining faults decreases.

The assumption that the size of faults is geometrically distributed is quite realistic. In a paper by Bishop and Pullen (1987) it has been observed that, approximately, the failure rate corresponding to each fault is exponentially distributed which is a continuous generalization of the geometric distribution. Also, the assumption of geometric distribution is not necessary and it is sufficient to assume that a randomly chosen fault has a size which is twice as large as the average size of the faults in order to make the power-type DFI model valid.

The above calculation can be generalized and if the i:th detected fault corresponds to the number of the input data which is about α times as large as the average size of the remaining faults, then

$$\lambda(i) = \phi(N_0-i+1)^\alpha$$

and this is the same as the failure intensity function for the general power-type DFI Markov model.

Assume now that we have a more favourable case where the largest of all remaining faults is removed each time the software is corrected. Under the assumption that the sizes of faults are geometrically distributed, we have that

$$\lambda(i) = \frac{\omega}{M} \sum_{j=1}^{N_0} M_j \approx \phi\left(b^{N_0-i+1}-1\right)$$

$$= \phi\left[e^{-\beta(N_0-i+1)}-1\right],$$

with some appropriate reparametrization. The term -1 is added in the above because of the condition $\lambda(N_0+1)=0$. Thus, we have obtained the exponential-type failure intensity function.

3.4. Models with time-dependent transition probability

In this section, we discuss some existing models which generalize the JM-model by assuming that the probability of state change is also time-dependent. An early model proposed by Schick and Wolverton (1978) together with a general formulation by Shanthikumar (1981) is presented.

3.4.1. The Schick-Wolverton model and its modifications

Schick and Wolverton (1978) studied a model using a time-dependent failure intensity function. The general assumptions made by the Schick-Wolverton model are the same as those for the JM-model except that the times between failures are independent with density function given by

$$f(t_i) = \phi(N_0-i+1)t_i \, exp\left\{\frac{-\phi(N_0-i+1)t_i^2}{2}\right\}, \quad i=1,2,\dots,N_0.$$

Here, N_0 is the number of initial faults and ϕ is another parameter.

Hence, the main difference between the Schick-Wolverton model and the JM-model is that the times between failures are not exponential, instead they are modelled by the so-called Rayleigh distribution which is a special case of the Weibull distribution. It can be seen as a Weibull formulation of the JM-model.

Note that this model can be derived by modifying the heuristic arguments in the previous sections. Assume that the test intensity ω is a linearly increasing function of the local time, i.e. $\omega(t_i)=ct_i$. By making the same assumptions about M_i as for the JM-model, that is by assuming that all M_i's are equal which is equivalent to the assumption that all faults are of the same size, then we get the Schick-Wolverton model.

In the Schick-Wolverton model the failure intensity function after detecting the i:th fault is

$$r(i,t_i) = \phi(N_0-i+1)t_i.$$

Note that the failure intensity function of the Schick-Wolverton model depends both on i, the number of removed faults and t_i, the time since the removal of last fault.

After the detection of the (i-1):th fault, the reliability function is given by

$$R(t_i) = exp\left\{ - \frac{\phi(N_0-i+1)t_i^2}{2}\right\},$$

and the corresponding mean time to next failure is given by

$$MTTF(i) = \left[\frac{\pi}{2\phi(N_0-i+1)}\right]^{1/2}.$$

The realism of the Schick-Wolverton model has been questioned, see Goel (1980b) for a summary of some discussions concerning the Schick-Wolverton model. The most essential problem here is that it is commonly accepted that the software failure intensity is not dependent on time, provided that the software is not changed and the test environment is completely random. Therefore, the assumption of a time-dependent failure rate function is not theoretically justified.

It should be pointed out that although this model has suffered from much critique for its unrealism for pure software, it is still worth considering in practice. An advantage of this model is that it can be useful in combined software and hardware system, because the time dependence can be used to describe some hardware failure behaviours.

Note that t_i in the Schick-Wolverton model is the current running time, not the cumulative test time. This model has been modified by Lipow (1975) which suggested that t_i in the Schick-Wolverton model can be replaced by a kind of running time,

$$\frac{1}{2}t_i + \sum_{j=1}^{i-1} t_j$$

and for this modified version the density function of the times between the (i-1):th and the i:th failures are

$$f(t_i) = \phi(N_0-i+1)\left(\frac{1}{2}t_i + \sum_{j=1}^{i-1} t_j\right)exp\left\{-\frac{1}{2}\phi(N_0-i+1)\left(\frac{1}{2}t_i + \sum_{j=1}^{i-1} t_j\right)^2\right\}.$$

The parameter estimation, both for the Schick-Wolverton model and its modified version, can be carried out by using the method of maximum likelihood. For the Schick-Wolverton model, the maximum likelihood estimates of N_0 and ϕ can be determined by

$$\phi = \sum_{i=1}^{n} \frac{2}{(N_0-i+1)\Sigma_{i=1}^{n}t_j^2},$$

$$N_0 = \frac{2n/\phi + \Sigma_{i=1}^{n}(i-1)t_i^2}{\Sigma_{i=1}^{n}t_i^2}.$$

See also Schick and Wolverton (1978) and Goel (1980b) for some further discussions concerning these models.

3.4.2. The Shanthikumar general Markov model

The JM-model can be generalized by using a general time-dependent transition probability function. A Markov formulation is presented by Shanthikumar (1981) and we briefly describe the model here.

Denoted by N(t) the number of faults that are detected and removed during time [0,t). Suppose that there are N_0 initial software faults and the model assumes that, after n faults are removed, the failure intensity of the software is given by

$$r(n,t) = \phi(t)(N_0 - n),$$

where $\phi(t)$ is a proportionality factor. Note that this model reduces to the JM-model if $\phi(t)$ is a constant independent of t.

Denote by $P_n(t)$ the probability distribution function of $N(t)$. Under the Markov assumption, we have that the forward Kolmogorov's differential equations are given as follows,

$$\frac{dP_0(t)}{dt} = -N_0\phi(t)P_0(t),$$

$$\frac{dP_n(t)}{dt} = (N_0-n+1)\phi(t)P_{n-1}(t) - (N_0-n)\phi(t)P_n(t); \quad 1 \le n \le N_0.$$

Using the boundary conditions $P_n(0)=0$, $n>0$ and $P_0(0)=1$, this system of differential equations can easily be solved and the solution is given by

$$P_n(t) = \left(\begin{array}{c} N_0 \\ n \end{array} \right) [a(t)]^{N_0-n}[1 - a(t)]^n; \quad 0 \le n \le N,$$

where a(t) is defined as

$$a(t) = exp\left\{ -\int_0^t \phi(x)dx \right\}.$$

A heuristic argument of this model, similar to that of the JM-model, is the following. Suppose that initially, there are N_0 software faults which can cause software failure and each fault contributes $\phi(t)$ to the failure intensity at time t. Then the total failure intensity is N_0 multiplied by $\phi(t)$. After removing the i:th fault, the failure intensity becomes $(N_0-i)\phi(t)$ which is the sum of the failure intensities from the remaining faults.

It should be noted that the assumption that all faults contribute the same amount to the failure intensity is still used here, hence this model suffers from the same critique as the JM-model. However, its time-dependent failure probability assumption does capture some desired properties of the nonhomogeneous Poisson process models which will be discussed in a later chapter.

For this general model the number of remaining faults at time t is Binomial distributed with parameter a(t), that is

$$P[N_0 - N(t) = k] = \left(\begin{array}{c} N_0 \\ k \end{array} \right) [a(t)]^k [1 - a(t)]^{N_0 - k}, \ 0 \le k \le N_0.$$

Other reliability and performance measures can be derived in a usual manner. The parameter estimation can also be carried out using the method of maximum likelihood. However, usually we have to have some further assumptions on $\phi(t)$.

3.5. Other generalizations of the JM-model

There are many other generalizations of the JM-model proposed in the existing literature. Some of them are discussed below. It can be noted that all of these models are suggested to remove some of the drawbacks associated with the JM-model by using more realistic assumptions.

3.5.1. An imperfect debugging model

The imperfect removal of a detected fault is a common situation in practice and most of the existing models do not take this into account. Goel, however, has suggested a generalization of the JM-model by assuming that each detected fault is removed with probability p, see e.g. Goel (1985). Hence, with probability q=1-p, a detected fault is not perfectly removed and the quantity q can be interpreted as the imperfect debugging probability.

The counting process of the cumulative number of detected faults at time t is modelled as a Markov counting process with transition probability depending on the probability of imperfect debugging. Still it is assumed that times between the transitions are exponential with a parameter which depends only on the number of remaining faults. After the occurrence of the (i-1):th failure, p(i-1) faults are removed on the average. Hence, approximately, there are $N_0 - p(i-1)$ faults left, where N_0 denotes the number of initial faults as before.

The failure intensity between the (i-1):th and the i:th failures is then

$$\lambda(i) = \phi[N_0 - p(i-1)].$$

Using this transition function, other reliability measures can be calculated as for the JM-model.

Note that the above intensity function can be rewritten as

$$\lambda(i) = \phi p\left[\frac{N_0}{p} - (i-1)\right],$$

and from this it can be seen that it is just the same as that for the JM-model with p replaced by $p\phi$ and N_0 replaced by N_0/p.

As a consequence, p, N_0 and ϕ are indistinguishable. But $p\phi$ and N_0/p can still be estimated similar to that for the parameters in the JM-model and N_0/p can be interpreted as the number of failures that will eventually occur. Another advantage of this imperfect debugging model is that when we know the probability of imperfect debugging, p, for example from the previous experience or by checking after correction, the number of initial faults N_0 and the constant of proportionality ϕ can be estimated.

3.5.2. A variable fault exposure coefficient model

The parameter ϕ in the JM-model which is a constant can be interpreted as a fault exposure coefficient (FEC). Bittanti et al. (1988b) presented an interesting model with variable FEC which has the same advantages as the DFI model discussed in Section 3.3. It also allows us to replace the assumption that all faults are equally exposed in testing by a more realistic one, that is a large number of trivial faults are detected earlier and the last faults are hard to detect which implies that the decrease of the failure intensity becomes less.

As before, the times between failures are assumed to be independent exponentially distributed random variables. The probability density function of the time between the j:th and the (j+1):th failure is,

$$f(t_j) = \lambda_j \exp\left(-\lambda_j t_j\right), \ j \geq 0,$$

where λ_j represents the average failure detection rate after removing the j:th fault.

The JM-model assumes that λ_j is the number of the remaining faults multiplied by a constant. The variable FEC model assumes that λ_j is the number of remaining faults multiplied by k(j), a function of j, that is

$$\lambda_j = k(j)\left(N_0 - j\right).$$

To allow a variable FEC, it is easiest to assume that FEC is a linear function of j, that is

$$k(j) = k_i + \frac{(k_f - k_i)j}{N_0}; \ k_i, k_f > 0.$$

The variable FEC model has thus three parameters: N_0 denotes the total number of faults in the software, k_i and k_f denote the initial and final values of the FEC, respectively.

Various patterns can be obtained using different values of k_i and k_f. It is also observed that if $k_f > 2k_i$, we have an S-shaped behaviour of the intensity curve which has been modelled using nonhomogeneous Poisson process models by many authors.

3.5.3. Other general Markov formulations

There are many other Markov models. Except for a few models, most existing models do not allow imperfect debugging or incorrect debugging and the Markov process is in fact a pure birth process. However, general birth-death process models can be formulated to deal with the probability of imperfect removal or even incorrect removal of software faults.

A birth-death process model for fault-counting processes is presented in Kremer (1983). This model assumes that the state of the software, the number of faults in the software which is also called the current fault content, can be modelled by a simple birth-death process. At time t, the failure intensity is equal to the product of the fault content and a given function $\lambda(t)$ which can be interpreted as the failure occurrence rate per fault.

When a failure occurs, the fault content is assumed to be reduced by 1 with probability p, and this is equivalent to the prefect removal of the fault causing that failure. The model is also capable dealing with the case of imperfect fault-removal by assuming that the fault content is not changed with probability q. Also the incorrect fault-removal which is often the case in practice is considered by assuming this probability to be r. The obvious equality is the following

$$p + q + r = 1.$$

This implies that we have a birth-death process with a birth rate $v(t) = r\lambda(t)$ and a death rate $\mu(t) = p\lambda(t)$.

However, in order to fit failure data and obtain further applicable results, assumptions on the function $\lambda(t)$ must be made. In Kremer (1983) several existing models are obtained by using the suitable $\lambda(t)$.

Denote by $\overline{N}(t)$ the number of remaining faults in the software at time t and let $p_n(t)$ be defined as the probability that $\overline{N}(t)=n$, $n=0,1,...,N_0$. From standard literature on stochastic processes, we obtain the forward Kolmogorov equations of this birth-death process as follows

$$p_n'(t) = (n-1)v(t)p_{n-1}(t) - n[v(t)+\mu(t)]p_n(t) + (n+1)\mu(t)p_{n+1}(t), \quad n \geq 0.$$

Generally, by inserting $v(t)$ and $\mu(t)$ and using the initial conditions

$$p_n(0) = \begin{cases} 1, & \text{if } n=N_0, \\ 0, & \text{otherwise;} \end{cases}$$

where N_0 is the number of initial faults, the differential equations can be solved, for example, by using the probability generating function suggested in Kremer (1983).

The solution of $\{p_n(t), n=0,1,\dots,N_0\}$ is given by

$$p_0(t) = [\alpha(t)]^{N_0},$$

$$p_n(t) = \sum_{i=0}^{min(N_0,n)} \binom{N_0}{i}\binom{N_0+n-i+1}{N_0-1}[\alpha(t)]^{N_0-i}[\beta(t)]^{n-i}\left[1-\alpha(t)-\beta(t)\right]^i, \; n>0;$$

where $\alpha(t)$, $\beta(t)$ are defined as

$$\alpha(t) = 1 - \frac{1}{e^{\rho(t)}+A(t)},$$

$$\beta(t) = 1 - \frac{e^{\rho(t)}}{e^{\rho(t)}+A(t)},$$

respectively, and

$$\rho(t) = (p-r)\int_0^t \lambda(t)\,dt,$$

$$A(t) = \int_0^t r\lambda(t)\,e^{\rho(t)}\,dt.$$

Using these results, other reliability measures can be derived, see Kremer (1983) for some further details. It can be noted here that the Kremer's Markov model is a generalization of several other existing models.

Another more general Markov formulation worth mentioning here is presented in Sumita and Shanthikumar (1986) where the authors suggested a multiple-failure Markov process model. The model assumed that X(t), the number of faults in the software at time t, is a Markov chain in continuous time with state space $\{0,1,\dots,N_0\}$. This model allows, by using a transition matrix, multiple fault introduction and fault removal. Several other models are in fact special cases of this model.

However, except for some special cases, the computation of $p_n(t)$, the probability that the software contains n faults, is not possible. In fact, complicated numerical procedures have usually been used. Interested readers are referred to the paper by Sumita and Shanthikumar (1986) where two algorithms are presented.

3.6. Markov models in system context

Usually, Markov process models are blackbox models in the sense that no information about the software system other than the failure time data is used. However, one usually has some data or descriptions about the structure of the software which can be incorporated. The behaviour of the software under the given environmental condition may also be known and it is a waste not using such information. In this section, we present some Markov models for which the structure of the software in a system context is utilized.

3.6.1. The Littlewood semi-Markov model

The Littlewood semi-Markov model incorporates the structure of the program, see Littlewood (1979b), by assuming that the software is composed of M modules. It is one of the first model of this kind. For the Littlewood semi-Markov model, transition between modules is assumed to have a semi-Markov property, that is, the probability of entering a new module is independent of the time spent in the previous module. When the program is in module i, failures then follow a Poisson process with parameter v_j. The failure probability of the interface between module i and j is assumed to be α_{ij}.

The distribution of the total number of failures observed during the time interval $[0,t)$, $N(t)$, is not easy to derive without further specification of the distributions of times spent in each module. However, some asymptotic results can be obtained. The asymptotic behaviour of $N(t)$, under the plausible assumption that individual failure rates are much smaller than the switching rates between modules, is asymptotically Poisson with a parameter equal to

$$\sum_{i=1}^{M} a_i v_i + \sum_{i=1}^{M} \sum_{j=1}^{M} b_{ij} \alpha_{ij},$$

where a_i represents the limiting proportion of time spent in module i and b_{ij} is the limiting frequency of i to j module transfers.

The problem in using this model in practice is that the parameters of the model have to be estimated. Usually, this requires a large amount of data which may give some information about these parameters. However, an important conclusion drawn from this model is that the Poisson assumption can be generally applicable to any modular software.

3.6.2. Some models of modular software

Similar to the Littlewood semi-Markov model, an interesting model called the user-oriented software reliability model is developed in Cheung (1980) where the user profile is incorporated into the reliability modelling. The model is a Markov model based on the reliability of each individual module and the intermodular transition probabilities as the user profile. Also the most critical module of the system can be determined by using sensitivity analysis techniques.

Assume that the software system is decomposed into a number of modules and it is also assumed that the reliabilities of the modules are independent and the transfer of control among program modules constitutes a Markov process, see Cheung (1980). Then the reliability of the system can be expressed as a function of the reliabilities of its modules and the user profile that is specified by the transitions between the modules.

Another recent Markov model of modular software is presented by Kubat (1989). Assume that the software is composed of M modules and there are K different tasks which the software is designed for. A task may require several modules to work and the same module can be used for different tasks. It is assumed that transitions between modules follow a Markov process. Knowing the individual failure intensity of each module, the transition probability and the execution characteristic, the reliability of the software system can be derived.

By the Markov assumptions, the probability that at least one failure occurs during the execution of task k while in module i is

$$1 - P_i(k) = \int_0^\infty e^{-\alpha_i t} g_{ik}(t)\, dt; \quad i=1,\dots,M; \; k=1,\dots,K;$$

where α_i is the failure intensity in module i and $g_{ik}(t)$ is the density function of the sojourn time during a visit in module i by task k. It can also be noted that $1-P_i(k)$ is just the Laplace transform of $g_{ik}(t)$.

Denote by $N_i(k)$ the number of times that task k will visit module i. Then the average number of visits in module i by task k is

$$a_i(k) = EN_i(k); \quad i=1,\dots,M; \; k=1,\dots,K;$$

and this can be obtained by solving

$$a_i(k) = q_i(k) + \sum_{j=1}^{M} p_{ji}(k)a_j(k); \quad i=1,\dots,M; \; k=1,\dots,K;$$

where $q_i(k)$ is the probability that the task k will first call module i and $p_{ij}(k)$ is the probability that the task k will call module j after executing in module i.

Using these quantities, the probability that there will be at least one failure when running for task k, $\pi(k)$, can be obtained as

$$\pi(k) = 1 - \prod_{i=1}^{M} [1 - P_i(k)]^{a_i(k)}; \quad k=1,\dots,K.$$

The system failure intensity may then be calculated by

$$\lambda_s = \sum_{k=1}^{K} r_k \pi(k),$$

where r_k is the arrival rate of task k.

It should be noted here that there is a well-developed theory in system reliability analysis. The application of the existing results is rear in software reliability analysis. The main reason is the lack of suitable data and this is an important area of further research.

3.6.3. Some availability models

Most of the existing software reliability models do not take repair time into consideration. Usually, it is assumed that after a failure the fault which has caused it is removed immediately while, in practice, it takes long time to find and correct a fault. Although failure data can be modified by counting the time of fault occurrence, this is a strong restriction when we are interested in the availability of the computer system.

Software availability is defined as the probability that the software is operating at time t. However, we are often interested in the system availability for which the software can be an essential part, hence, availability models usually combine both software and hardware failures, see e.g. Sumita and Masuda (1986), Goyal and Lavenberg (1987) and Ohtera et al. (1990). Trivedi and Shooman (1982) studied an availability model of the software based on a Markov chain model. We give a brief description about this model in the following as it is closely related to the topics discussed in this chapter.

According to Trivedi and Shooman (1982), the system states are divided into up and down state according to whether the software is functioning or not. Initially, the system is assumed to be in an up state, that is, it is assumed to be functioning at t=0. When a software failure occurs, the system is shut down and enters the down state. The fault which has caused this failure is then detected and removed before the system begins to function again. Both the functioning times and repair times are assumed to be random quantities and the process is modelled by a Markov process. A failure rate function $\lambda(t)$ is used to represent the frequency of transition from up to down state and another repair rate function $\mu(t)$ represents the frequency of transition from the down to up state.

Denote by $p_i(t)$, i=n,n-1,..., the probability that the software is in the i:th functioning state at time t. Similarly, we denote by $q_i(t)$, i=m,m-1,..., the probability that the software is in the i:th down state at time t. Given the failure rate function $\lambda(t)$ and the repair function $\mu(t)$, the state probabilities can be obtained by solving the following differential equations,

$$p_n'(t) = -\lambda(t)\,p_n(t),$$

$$p_{n-i}'(t) = -\lambda(t)\,p_{n-i}(t) + \mu(t)\,q_{m-i+1}(t), \quad i=0,1,2,\dots;$$

and

$$q_{m-i}'(t) = -\mu(t)\,q_{m-i}(t) + \lambda(t)\,p_{n-i}(t), \quad i=0,1,2,\dots.$$

Together with the initial conditions given by

$$p_n(0) = 1 \ \ and \ \ p_k(0)=0 \ \ for \ \ k\neq n;$$

the above equation system can be solved and the solution is given by

$$p_{n-i}(t) = \left(\frac{\lambda\mu}{\mu-\lambda}\right)^i e^{-\lambda t} \sum_{j=0}^{i} \frac{t^{i-j}\left\{(-1)^{i+1}c_{ij}e^{-(\mu-\lambda)t} + (-1)^j d_{ij}\right\}}{(\mu-\lambda)(i-j)!},$$

where

$$c_{ij} = \left\{ \begin{array}{ll} 0, & for \ j=0, \\ 1, & for \ j=1, \\ \dbinom{i+j-1}{j-1}, & otherwise; \end{array} \right.$$

and

$$d_{ij} = \left\{ \begin{array}{ll} 1, & for \ j=0, \\ \dbinom{i+j-1}{j-1}, & otherwise; \end{array} \right.$$

and similarly we get

$$p_{m-i}(t) = \frac{1}{\mu}\left(\frac{\lambda\mu}{\mu-\lambda}\right)^{i+1} e^{-\lambda t} \sum_{j=0}^{i} \frac{c_{ij+1} t^{i-j}\{(-1)^{i+1} e^{-(\mu-\lambda)t} + (-1)^j\}}{(\mu-\lambda)(i-j)!}.$$

Then the availability of the software can be calculated by summing up all $p_i(t)$, that is

$$A(t) = p_n(t) + p_{n-1}(t) + \dots = \sum_{k=0}^{\infty} p_{n-k}(t).$$

The simplest case is when the failure rate and repair rate are constant functions. Other possible functions for $\lambda(t)$ and $\mu(t)$ are

$$\lambda(t) = exp\{a + br^t\},$$

$$\mu(t) = \frac{1}{1 + exp\{a + br^t\}}.$$

where a, b and r are parameters.

Availability models are widely studied in hardware reliability in order to obtain cost-effective replacement policy. For a software system the application of these models is limited since the up and down states of a software is not obvious. The software can still be used while repair of it is taking place.

3.7. Bibliographic notes

The model by Jelinski and Moranda (1972) has been widely studied. Many existing software reliability models are generalizations of that model. In Shooman (1972) a similar model by using a man-power related time scale has been studied.

Problems concerning the maximum likelihood estimates of the JM-model have been studied by Forman and Singpurwalla (1977), (1979), Littlewood (1981b), Joe and Reid (1985), Spreij (1985), Wright and Hazelhurst (1988), Xie and Åkerlund (1989) and Huang (1990).

Bayesian generalization of the JM-model will be discussed in Section 6.3. See also bibliographic notes at the end of Chapter 6.

Xie and Bergman (1988) proposed a general Markov formulation by assuming that fault-detection probability depends on the size of fault which leads to a general Markov model with decreasing jump intensity function. Shanthikumar (1981) also studied another type of generalization by using time-dependent transition probability function. Kremer (1983) presented a general model for the fault-counting process using a birth-death formulation which incorporates both fault-removal and fault-introduction. A general model similar to this may also be found in Stålhane and Lindqvist (1989) and Trachtenberg (1990).

Other generalizations and modifications of the JM-model can be found in Moranda (1975), (1981), Schick and Wolverton (1978), Goel (1980), Trachtenberg (1985), Xie (1987) and Bittanti et al. (1988b).

Models for imperfect debugging related to the JM-model have been studied in Goel (1985) and Ohba and Chou (1989). See also other models by Kremer (1983), Sumita and Shanthikumar (1986), Kapur and Garg (1990b), (1991b).

Markov models in a system context, especially, models for modular software are considered in Littlewood (1979b), Cheung (1980), Hecht and Hecht (1986), Masuda et al. (1989), Kubat (1989) and Ho et al. (1989).

Availability models are studied in Trivedi and Shooman (1975), Goyal and Lavenberg (1987), Sumita and Masuda (1986) and Ohtera et al. (1990c).

4

Nonhomogeneous Poisson Process (NHPP) Models

In this chapter, we present some existing software reliability models for which failure processes are described by nonhomogeneous Poisson processes. After a brief introduction to NHPP models and their properties the Goel-Okumoto model which is the most well-known NHPP model is discussed in detail in Section 4.2. Some typical S-shaped NHPP models which are generalizations of the GO-model and the Musa execution time model together with some modifications are discussed in Section 4.3 and Section 4.4, respectively. In Section 4.5 other existing NHPP models useful to describe the software failure process in different situations are presented. Finally, we give some general comments on NHPP models and some bibliographic notes are also provided.

4.1. General theory of NHPP modelling

As a general class of well-developed stochastic process models in reliability engineering, nonhomogeneous Poisson process models have been successfully used in studying hardware reliability problems. NHPP models are especially useful to describe failure processes which possess certain trends such as reliability growth or deterioration.

Application of NHPP models to software reliability analysis is then easily implemented. The cumulative number of software failures up to time t, N(t), can be described by a NHPP and many existing software reliability models also belong to this class.

For the counting process {N(t),t≥0} modelled by NHPP, N(t) follows a Poisson distribution with parameter m(t), that is, the probability that N(t) is a given integer n is expressed by

$$P\{N(t){=}n\} = \frac{[m(t)]^n}{n!}\, e^{-m(t)}, \;\; n{=}0,1,2,\dots .$$

In the above m(t) is called the mean value function. The function m(t) describes the expected cumulative number of failures in [0,t). Hence, m(t) is a very useful descriptive measure of the failure behaviour.

The underlying assumptions of the NHPP are:

(1) $N(0) = 0$,
(2) $\{N(t),\, t{\geq}0\}$ has independent increments,
(3) $P\{N(t{+}h){-}N(t){=}1\} = \lambda(t) + o(h)$,
(4) $P\{N(t{+}h){-}N(t){\geq}2\} = o(h)$.

In the above o(h) denotes a quantity which tends to zero for small h. The function $\lambda(t)$ which is called the instantaneous failure intensity is defined as

$$\lambda(t) = \underset{\Delta t \to 0_+}{Lim}\; \frac{P\{N(t{+}\Delta t){-}N(t){>}0\}}{\Delta t}.$$

Given $\lambda(t)$, the mean value function m(t)=EN(t) satisfies

$$m(t) = \int_0^t \lambda(s)ds.$$

Inversely, knowing m(t), the failure intensity at time t can be obtained as

$$\lambda(t) = \frac{dm(t)}{dt}.$$

Generally, by using different nondecreasing functions m(t), we get different NHPP models. In the most simple case for which $\lambda(t)$ is constant, the NHPP becomes a homogeneous Poisson process which has a mean value function as t multiplied by constant .

Due to the great variability of the mean value functions, NHPP models have been widely studied in the existing literature. One of the first NHPP models is suggested by Schneidewind (1975). The most well-known NHPP model is the model studied in Goel and Okumoto (1979) which later on, has been further generalized and modified by various authors in order to improve the goodness-of-fit to real software failure data.

Define the number of remaining software faults at time t by $\overline{N}(t)$ and we have that

$$\overline{N}(t) = N(\infty) - N(t),$$

where $N(\infty)$ is the number of faults which can be detected by infinite time of testing.

It follows from the standard theory of NHPP that the distribution of $\overline{N}(t)$ is Poisson with parameter $m(\infty)-m(t)$, that is

$$P\{\overline{N}(t)=k\} = \frac{[m(\infty)-m(t)]^k}{n!} exp\{m(\infty)-m(t)\}, \quad k=0,1,2,\dots.$$

The reliability function at time t_0 is exponential given by

$$R(t|t_0) = exp\{-[m(t+t_0)-m(t_0)]\}.$$

Usually, m(t) contains some unknown parameters. The estimation of them is generally carried out by using the method of maximum likelihood or the method of least squares, see e.g. Schneidewind (1975).

Denote by n_i the number of faults detected in time interval $[s_{i-1}, s_i)$, where $0=s_0<s_1<s_2<...<s_n$ and s_i, $i\geq0$, are the running times since the software testing begins. The likelihood function for the NHPP model with mean value function m(t) is the following

$$L(n_1,n_2,...,n_k) = \prod_{i=1}^{k} \frac{[m(s_{i-1})-m(s_i)]^{n_i} exp\{m(s_{i-1})-m(s_i)\}}{n_i!}.$$

The parameters in m(t) can then be estimated by maximizing this likelihood function. Usually, numerical procedures have to be used in solving the likelihood equations.

It should be pointed out here that NHPP has many desirable properties. NHPP's are closed under superposition, that is, the sum of a number of NHPP's is also a NHPP. Generally, we may just mix the failure time data from different failure processes assumed to be NHPP and get an overall NHPP with a mean value function which is the sum of the mean value functions of the underlying NHPP's.

Any NHPP can be transformed to a homogeneous Poisson process through an appropriate time-transformation. From the general theory of NHPP, it is well-known that if $\{N(t), t \geq 0\}$ is a NHPP with mean value function m(t), then the time-transformed process $N^*(t)$ defined as

$$N^*(t) = N(a(t)), \ t \geq 0;$$

is also NHPP. The mean value function of the NHPP $\{N^*(t), t \geq 0\}$ is

$$m^*(t) = m(a(t)), \ t \geq 0.$$

Especially, if $a(t) = m^{-1}(t)$, we have that the time-transformed process becomes a homogeneous Poisson process with rate one, i.e. the mean value function is equal to t.

4.2. The Goel-Okumoto (GO) model

In 1979, Goel and Okumoto presented a simple model for the description of software failure process by assuming that the cumulative failure process is NHPP with a simple mean value function. Although NHPP models have been studied before, see e.g. Schneidewind (1975), it is the GO-model that later has had a strong influence on the software reliability modelling history. In this section, we present this model in detail together with a simple generalization.

4.2.1. Model assumptions and some properties

The general assumptions of the GO-model are

(1) The cumulative number of faults detected at time t follows a Poisson distribution.

(2) All faults are independent and have the same chance of being detected.

(3) All detected faults are removed immediately and no new faults are introduced.

Specifically, the GO-model assumes that the failure process is modelled by an NHPP model with mean value function m(t) given by

$$m(t) = a\left(1 - e^{-bt}\right), \ a>0, \ b>0;$$

where a and b are parameters to be determined using collected failure data. A simple heuristic derivation of this mean value function will be given in Section 4.2.2.

Note that for this model we have

$$m(\infty) = a \ \text{ and } \ m(0) = 0.$$

Since m(∞) is the expected number of faults which will eventually be detected, the parameter a is then the final number of faults that can be detected by the testing process. The quantity b which is a constant of proportionality, can be interpreted as the failure occurrence rate per fault.

The intensity function λ(t) defined as the derivative of m(t) is then

$$\lambda(t) = \frac{dm(t)}{dt} = abe^{-bt}.$$

The expected number of remaining faults at time t,

$$E\overline{N}(t) = E\left[N(\infty) - N(t)\right],$$

may then be calculated as follows

$$E\overline{N}(t) = m(\infty) - m(t) = a - a(1-e^{-bt}) = ae^{-bt}.$$

Hence, the expected number of remaining faults $\overline{EN}(t)$ is an exponentially decreasing function of t. When the parameters a and b are estimated using collected data, see Section 4.2.3 for the maximum likelihood estimation of the parameters of the GO-model, the expected number of remaining faults can easily be calculated.

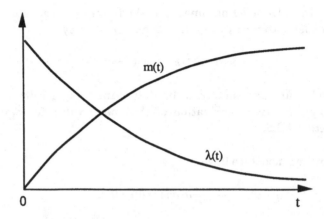

Figure 4.1. The shape of the intensity function and the mean value function for the GO-model.

It can be shown that, given that the last failure occurs at time s, the reliability function is

$$R(t|s) = exp\left\{-a(e^{-bs} - e^{-b(s+t)})\right\}.$$

It can be noted here that this model assumes that the number of initial faults is a random quantity. A unification approach of the GO-model and the JM-model has been proposed in Langberg and Singpurwalla (1985) where some Bayesian formulations are found.

Both the GO-model and the JM-model give the exponentially decreasing number of remaining faults. It can be shown that these two models cannot be distinguished using only one realization from each model. However, the models are different because the JM-model assumes a discrete change of the failure intensity at the time of the removal of a fault while the GO-model assumes a continuous failure intensity function over the whole time domain.

4.2.2. A heuristic derivation of the GO-model

The GO-model can be derived under some simple assumptions. Treat the cumulative number of software faults detected by time t, N(t), as a continuous random variable and assume that the stochastic process {N(t),t≥0} can be described by an NHPP with mean value function m(t). Assume that m(t) is a bounded, nondecreasing function of t and m(0)=0. Then the following arguments may lead to the form of the mean value function of the GO-model.

Suppose that the expected number of faults detected in a time interval [t,t+Δt) is proportional to the number of remaining faults, we have that,

$$m(t+\Delta t) = b[a-m(t)]\Delta t,$$

where b is a constant of proportionality.

The above difference equation can be transformed into a differential equation. Divide both sides by Δt and take limits by letting Δt tend to zero, we get the following equation,

$$m'(t) = ab - bm(t).$$

It can easily be verified that the solution of this differential equation, together with the initial condition m(0)=0, is

$$m(t) = a(1-e^{-bt}),$$

and this is just the underlying mean value function of the GO-model.

It should be pointed out here that both the GO-model and the JM-model make the assumption that all faults contribute the same amount to the software failure intensity which is unrealistic for both models. The modifications of the JM-model by using other more realistic assumptions have been studied by many authors. There are also some generalizations of the GO-model which have been proposed to modify this assumption which will be discussed in later sections.

4.2.3. Parameter estimation of the GO-model

The estimation of model parameters a and b can be carried out by maximizing the likelihood function. In the following, we assume that the failure data are grouped and its modification to the ungrouped case is trivial.

Inserting the value of $m(t_i)$ for all i into the likelihood function for the general NHPP model, we get that the likelihood function of the parameters a and b is

$$L(n_1, n_2, ..., n_k) = \prod_{i=1}^{k} \frac{\left[a(e^{-bs_{i-1}} - e^{-bs_i})\right]^{n_i} exp\{a(e^{-bs_{i-1}} - e^{-bs_i})\}}{n_i!}.$$

The natural logarithm of this likelihood function is

$$lnL = ln\left\{ \prod_{i=1}^{k} \frac{\left[a(e^{-bs_{i-1}} - e^{-bs_i})\right]^{n_i} exp\{a(e^{-bs_{i-1}} - e^{-bs_i})\}}{n_i!} \right\}$$

$$= \sum_{i=1}^{k} n_i \, lna + \sum_{i=1}^{k} n_i \, ln\left(e^{-bs_{i-1}} - e^{-bs_i}\right) + \sum_{i=1}^{k} a\left(e^{-bs_{i-1}} - e^{-bs_i}\right) - \sum_{i=1}^{k} ln\left(n_i!\right).$$

Denote by n the total number of detected faults, that is

$$n = \sum_{i=1}^{k} n_i.$$

By taking the partial derivatives of the log-likelihood function with respect to a and b and equating them to zero, that is

$$\frac{\partial lnL}{\partial a} = \frac{\partial lnL}{\partial b} = 0,$$

we get the following equations for solving a and b,

$$n - a(1 - e^{-bs_k}) = 0,$$

$$\sum_{i=1}^{k} \frac{n_i \left(s_i e^{-bs_{i-1}} - s_{i-1} e^{-bs_i} \right)}{e^{-bs_{i-1}} - e^{-bs_i}} - a s_k e^{-bs_k} = 0.$$

The estimate of a may easily be found as

$$a = \frac{n}{1 - e^{-bs_k}},$$

and after inserting this expression into the second of the likelihood equation above, the estimate of b can be calculated by solving the following

$$\sum_{i=1}^{k} \frac{n_i \left(s_i e^{-bs_{i-1}} - s_{i-1} e^{-bs_i} \right)}{e^{-bs_{i-1}} - e^{-bs_i}} - \frac{n s_k e^{-bs_k}}{1 - e^{-bs_k}} = 0.$$

. Usually, this equation has to be solved numerically by using some numerical procedures. It can also be shown that the estimates are asymptotically normal and a confidence region can easily be established.

4.2.4. A simple generalization

Because NHPP models are characterized by the mean value function m(t), other NHPP models can be obtained by using other mean value functions and there are many NHPP models proposed by various authors. Here, we give a simple example which is a direct generalization of the GO-model.

It has been observed that the software failure intensity increases slightly at the beginning and then it begins to decrease. In order to describe this phenomenon, Goel (see Goel, 1985) proposed a simple generalization of the GO-model. The only difference between the Goel´s generalized NHPP model and the GO-model is that the mean value function of the generalized NHPP model is given by

$$m(t) = a[1 - exp(-bt^c)].$$

As before, a is the expected number of faults in the software, b is a kind of scale parameter which reflects the intensity of testing and c is another parameter which can be interpreted as the test quality. The failure intensity function of this model is

$$\lambda(t) = \frac{dm(t)}{dt} = abct^{c-1} exp\{-bt^c\}.$$

This generalized model is a three-parameter model and with an appropriate value of the third parameter, it can give better goodness-of-fit than the original model. However, by adding a new parameter, the estimation involving more numerical procedures becomes more difficult and due to the lack of a direct argument of this model, the applicability of this model has been limited. In the next section we will present some other models which are also able to handle the case when we have an increasing-then-decreasing failure intensity curve. Anyhow, this simple generalization provides us some general ideas about how to construct new NHPP models.

4.3. S-shaped NHPP model

The mean value function of the GO-model is exponential-shaped. Based on the experience, it is observed that the curve of the cumulative number of faults is often S-shaped relatively to the exponential-shaped mean value function which means that the curve crosses the exponential curve from below and the crossing occurs once and only once. A number of generalizations or modifications are thus proposed, mostly by Japanese researchers, see Ohba et al. (1982) and Yamada et al. (1984c) where some heuristic reasons of the occurrence of S-shapedness are also provided.

Generally, the S-shapedness can be explained by the fact that faults are neither independent nor of the same size. At the beginning of the testing, some faults are "covered" by other faults and before these faults are detected and removed, the covered faults cannot be detected. Hence, removing a detected fault at the beginning does not decrease the failure intensity very much since the same test data will still lead to a failure caused by other "covered" faults. In a later phase, large faults are already removed and the remaining faults have small size so that the fault-detection rate is of moderate size. Also because there are not many faults left in the software, the coverage has no significant effect at the end of the testing phase.

Another reason of the S-shaped behaviour is also proposed by Yamada et al. (1984c) as the following. The software reliability testing usually involves a learning process by which people become familiar with the software and the test tools. Their skills improve gradually and test effectiveness also increases. Hence, there is a tendency that the cumulative number of failures have an S-shaped form which implies that the increase of the reliability at the beginning is only of modest size due to the low test effectiveness, then the reliability increases quickly and later the improvement slows down again since most of the faults are already removed.

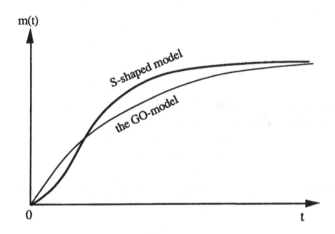

Figure 4.2. The S-shaped failure intensity function.

Several different S-shaped NHPP models have been proposed in the existing literature, especially by Japanese researchers. The most interesting ones are the delayed S-shaped NHPP model and the inflected S-shaped NHPP model.

The mean value function of the *delayed S-shaped NHPP* model is

$$m(t) = a[1 - (1 + bt)e^{-bt}]; \quad b > 0.$$

This is a two-parameter S-shaped curve with parameter a denoting the number of faults to be detected and b corresponding to a failure detection rate. The corresponding intensity function of this delayed S-shaped NHPP model is

$$\lambda(t) = \frac{dm(t)}{dt} = ab(1 + bt)e^{-bt} - abe^{-bt} = ab^2te^{-bt}.$$

The expected number of remaining faults EN(t) at time t is then

$$m(\infty) - m(t) = a - a[1 - (1 + bt)e^{-bt}] = a(1 + bt)e^{-bt}.$$

Another general model of this kind is proposed in Schagen (1987), where the expected number of faults detected by time t is modelled by the following mean value function

$$m(t) = \alpha\left[1 - e^{-\lambda_1 t} - \frac{\lambda_2(e^{-\lambda_1 t} - e^{-\lambda_2 t})}{\lambda_2 - \lambda_1}\right].$$

In the above, α, λ_1 and λ_2 are the model parameters. It can be seen that if $\lambda_1 = \lambda_2$, then we have the limiting case

$$m(t) = a[1 - (1 + \lambda_1 t)e^{-\lambda_1 t}],$$

which is the same as that for the delayed S-shaped NHPP model with $a = \alpha$ and $b = \lambda_1$.

The mean value function of the *inflected S-shaped NHPP* model is

$$m(t) = \frac{a(1 - e^{-bt})}{1 + ce^{-bt}}; \quad b > 0, c > 0.$$

In the above a is again the total number of faults to be detected while b and c are called the failure detection rate and the inflection factor, respectively. The intensity function of this inflected S-shaped NHPP model can easily be derived as follows,

$$\lambda(t) = \frac{dm(t)}{dt} = \frac{abe^{-bt}\left(1+ce^{-bt}\right)+abce^{-bt}\left(1-e^{-bt}\right)}{\left(1+ce^{-bt}\right)^2}$$

$$= \frac{abe^{-bt}+abce^{-bt}}{\left(1+ce^{-bt}\right)^2} = \frac{ab(1+c)e^{-bt}}{\left(1+ce^{-bt}\right)^2}.$$

Similarly, as for the delayed S-shaped NHPP model, we may obtain the expected number of remaining faults EN(t) at time t as follows

$$m(\infty) - m(t) = a - \frac{a\left(1-e^{-bt}\right)}{1+ce^{-bt}} = \frac{a(1+c)e^{-bt}}{1+ce^{-bt}}.$$

Some heuristic arguments for this mean value function are presented in Ohba et al. (1982). Using this mean value function, the parameters can be estimated using maximum likelihood method. Interested readers are referred to that paper.

4.4. The Musa execution time model and generalizations

Musa (1975) presented a theory of software reliability analysis based on the execution time. Some further extensions and modifications of the Musa´s execution time model have also been suggested and studied. Since software testing is in a sense much more uniform in execution time than in calendar time, execution time is a better measure of time and it should be used as the measure of time whenever it is possible.

4.4.1. The basic execution time model

Denote by N_0 and $\mu(\tau)$ the number of initial faults in the software and the number of faults corrected after τ amount of testing measured in execution time, respectively. In this section, we will use τ to denote the cumulative computer execution time which is a common notation in the existing literature. For the Musa´s basic execution time model, see e.g. Musa et al. (1987), the failure rate function at the execution time τ, $\lambda(\tau)$, is assumed to be proportional to the number of remaining faults in the software. That is, the following relation is valid,

$$\lambda(\tau) = fK[N_0 - \mu(\tau)],$$

where f and K are parameters related to the testing phase. According to Musa (1975), the quantity f can be taken as the linear execution frequency in the way that the average instruction execution rate divided by the total number of instructions in the program and K is a fault exposure ratio which relates fault exposure frequency to the linear execution frequency.

Suppose that the fault correction rate is proportional to the failure occurrence rate, we have then

$$\frac{d\mu(\tau)}{d\tau} = BC\lambda(\tau),$$

where B is defined as the fault reduction factor and C is called the testing compression factor. The testing compression factor, which takes into account the greater stress that is placed on the program to uncover program faults during the testing phase in contrast to the operational phase, is the average ratio of fault-detection rate during the testing to that during the usage.

Combining the above equalities, we get that

$$\frac{d\mu(\tau)}{d\tau} = BC\lambda(\tau) = BCfK[N_0 - \mu(\tau)].$$

This is a differential equation and it can be written as

$$\mu'(\tau) + BCfK\mu(\tau) - BCfKN_0 = 0.$$

By the initial condition $\mu(\tau)=0$ for $\tau=0$, we get that the solution of the above differential equation is

$$\mu(\tau) = N_0\left(1 - e^{-BCfK\tau}\right).$$

The above function for $\mu(\tau)$ is just the mean value function of the Musa basic execution time model. Using this mean value function and the theory of NHPP, other analytical results may easily be obtained.

If, instead of the number of detected faults, we want to model the failure process by counting the cumulative number of failures at execution time τ, $v(\tau)$, similar results can be obtained and by using the fault reduction factor B, we get

$$v(\tau) = M_0\left(1 - e^{-BC_fK\tau}\right),$$

where $M_0 = N_0/B$.

4.4.2. The logarithmic Poisson execution time model

Musa and Okumoto (1984a) presented another model which is called logarithmic Poisson execution time model by considering the possibility of infinite number of faults. Times are stressed to be in terms of execution time and the failure process is also assumed to be a NHPP.

The main assumption of this model is that the failure intensity decreases exponentially as a function of the number of removed faults. The expression of this assumption is, using the notations of the Musa's execution time theory,

$$\lambda(\tau) = \lambda_0 e^{-\varphi\mu(\tau)},$$

where λ_0 is the initial failure intensity and φ is called the failure intensity decay parameter.

Using this assumption, together with the relation between the expected number of removed faults and the failure intensity, that is,

$$\frac{d\mu(\tau)}{d\tau} = \lambda(\tau),$$

we get the following differential equation,

$$\mu'(\tau) = \lambda_0 e^{-\varphi\mu(\tau)}.$$

By using the initial condition $\mu(0)=0$, this equation can be solved and the solution is given by

$$\mu(\tau) = \frac{1}{\varphi} \ln(\lambda_0 \varphi \tau + 1).$$

This is just the mean value function of the logarithmic Poisson execution time model whose name stems from the fact that the expected number of failures $\mu(\tau)$ is a logarithmic function of τ. An example of such a function is displayed in Figure 4.3 together with a curve of the mean value function of Musa's basic execution time model. Note that the main difference between these two mean value functions is that the value of $\mu(\tau)$ of the logarithmic execution time models tends to infinity for large τ while a limiting value exists for the basic execution time model.

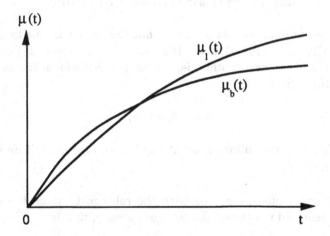

Figure 4.3. The mean value function of the Musa's basic execution time model, $\mu_b(t)$, and the logarithmic Poisson execution time model, $\mu_l(t)$.

The corresponding failure intensity at the execution time τ is given by

$$\lambda(\tau) = \lambda_0 e^{-\varphi \mu(\tau)} = \frac{\lambda_0}{\lambda_0 \varphi \tau + 1}.$$

Using the mean value function we get that the reliability function at time τ_0 is

$$R(\tau|\tau_0) = \left[\frac{\lambda_0 \varphi \tau + 1}{\lambda_0 \varphi(\tau + \tau_0) + 1} \right]^{1/\varphi}, \quad \tau \geq 0.$$

and, by using other general theories of NHPP models, other reliability measures can be obtained, see Musa and Okumoto (1984a).

4.4.3. Notes on applying execution time models

In order to apply execution time models, it is necessary to have some information about the values of various parameters which can be obtained from an initial estimation using a simple model. Usually, the values of the parameters are taken from other similar projects and re-estimation of the parameters can also be possible as the testing progresses. However, these parameters depend on many other factors and they may vary from company to company and from software to software.

Musa's basic model is similar to the GO-model from a probabilistic point of view. However, execution time models are interesting mainly due to the following two reasons:

(1) the execution time model stresses the importance of using the execution time instead of calendar time, and it is possible to combine these time measures.

(2) these models can be used in studying testing-effort and this is helpful for software managers to carry out development planning.

The execution time models are very useful in practice when we have the recorded failure data in computer execution time. Usually, it is hard to collect these data and there are only a few sets of data in open literature. Musa (1979a) published a data set which was carefully collected and consisted of execution time data for many different projects. It is the first of this kind and there is a need for a common standard for the data collection.

Execution time can be directly incorporated into many other models such as the JM-model although, in order to take some practical measures into account, some modification is necessary. Shooman (1972) discussed how the man-power data can be used and how a reliability model should be constructed in this case.

Sometimes both calendar time component and execution time component have to be considered and this has been an important topic in many papers by Musa, see e.g. Musa (1979b) and Musa and Okumoto (1984a). Execution time is useful to obtain more accurate estimation of software reliability, but from the management point of view, calender time models are more efficient for the allocation of testing resource and for the determination of optimum release time. It is possible to combine calendar time and execution time for many different software reliability models. Govil (1984) provided some indication of how execution time concept can be incorporated into some existing software reliability models.

4.5. Other NHPP models

Since NHPP models have been widely studied in hardware reliability analysis, especially in studying reliability growth phenomena, there are many other models proposed by adapting existing NHPP models to describe software failure behaviour. Some of those NHPP models together with some other interesting modifications are briefly presented in this section.

4.5.1. Some reliability growth models

Reliability growth which is a common phenomenon in hardware design process has been studied for a long time. Due to the similarity between software reliability behaviour and hardware design improvement, many existing reliability growth models can directly be used. Sometimes the failure intensity of a repairable systems is called ROCOF (Rate Of oCcurrence Of Failures).

Here, we will briefly describe some existing reliability growth models which have been used in software reliability context. The first is the Duane model interpreted as a NHPP model for reliability growth. A modification of this model due to Littlewood (1984) is also presented. Then the logistic growth model and the Gompertz growth model are discussed.

The Duane model which is also referred to as *the Weibull process model* assumes that the mean value function satisfies

$$m(t) = \left(\frac{t}{\alpha}\right)^{\beta}, \quad \alpha > 0, \beta > 0.$$

In the above, α and β are parameters which can be estimated by using collected failure data. The ROCOF at time t, $\lambda(t)$, is

$$\lambda(t) = \frac{dm(t)}{dt} = \frac{\beta}{\alpha}\left(\frac{t}{\alpha}\right)^{\beta-1}, \quad \alpha > 0, \beta > 0.$$

One of the most important advantages of the Duane reliability growth model is that if we plot the cumulative number of failure versus the cumulative testing time on a log-log-scaled paper, the plotted points tends to be close to a straight line if the model is valid. This can be seen from the fact that the relation between m(t) and t can be rewritten as

$$lnm(t) = \beta ln(t/\alpha) = \beta lnt - \beta ln\alpha = a + blnt,$$

with

$$a = -\beta ln\alpha \text{ and } b = \beta.$$

Hence, lnm(t) is a linear function of lnt and due to this linear relation, the parameters α and β may be estimated graphically and the model validity can easily be verified.

Some of the disadvantages of the Duane model are that it gives an infinite ROCOF at time zero and it gives zero ROCOF at time infinity. Littlewood (1984) proposed a modified version of the Duane model by assuming the mean value function of *the modified Duane model* to be

$$m(t) = k\left[1 - \left(\frac{\alpha}{\alpha+t}\right)^{\beta}\right], \quad \alpha > 0, \beta > 0, k > 0.$$

The parameter k can be interpreted as the number of faults eventually to be detected. The corresponding ROCOF is

$$\lambda(t) = m'(t) = k\beta\alpha^{\beta}(\alpha + t)^{-1-\beta}, \quad \alpha>0, \ \beta>0, \ k>0.$$

Note that for this modification, the ROCOF at time zero is equal to $k\beta/\alpha$ which is finite and it tends to zero as t tends to infinity.

Since software reliability can be treated as a growth process, models developed to predict hardware reliability growth, economic growth, population growth, etc., can also be applied. Applications of growth models such as the logistic curve and the Gompertz growth curve model, see e.g. Yamada and Osaki (1985c) have been reported.

These models, as it is for the Duane model, simply fit the cumulative number of detected faults at a given time by a function of known form. *The logistic growth curve* is given by

$$m(t) = \frac{k}{1 + ae^{-bt}}, \quad a>0, \ b>0, \ k>0,$$

where a, b and k are constant parameters which can be estimated by fitting the failure data. The parameter k in this logistic model can be interpreted as the expected number of initial faults in the software because it can easily be shown that $m(\infty)=k$.

For *the Gompertz growth curve* model, the expected cumulative number of detected faults at time t is given by

$$m(t) = ka^{b^t}, \quad 0<a, \ b<1, \ k>0.$$

Note that, since b<1, we have that

$$m(\infty) = ka^{b^{\infty}} = ka^0 = k.$$

Hence, for this model, k may also be interpreted as the expected number of initial faults in the software while a and b are other constants and all these parameters can be estimated by fitting the failure data.

4.5.2. NHPP models using testing-effort

The testing phase is an important and expensive part during the development of software products. The behaviour of the testing resource expenditures over the testing period can be observed as a consumption curve of testing-effort and the increase in reliability is strongly dependent on the allocated testing-effort. Software reliability models may also be developed by incorporating some testing-effort models.

As usual, denote by N(t) the cumulative number of faults detected and corrected at time t. The NHPP model assumes that

$$P\{N(t)=n\} = \frac{[m(t)]^n}{n!}e^{-m(t)}; \quad n \geq 0,$$

where m(t) is the mean value function. Testing-effort dependent software reliability models generally assume that m(t) depends on a testing-effort function which can be incorporated in order to get a more reasonable model.

Yamada et al. (1986b) presented a testing-effort dependent software reliability growth model for which the software fault detection process is modelled by an NHPP based on the one by Goel and Okumoto (1979). It assumes that the fault-detection rate is proportional to the number of remaining software faults and the constant of proportionality depends on the current testing-effort expenditure.

Denote by w(t) the testing-effort spent at time t, a relationship between m(t) and w(t) is provided with by Yamada and Ohtera (1990)

$$m(t) = a[1 - e^{-rW(t)}]; \quad 0 < r < 1, a > 0,$$

where a is the expected number of initial faults and r is the fault detection rate, interpreted as the per unit testing-effort at testing time t. In the above W(t) is defined as

$$W(t) = \int_0^t w(s)ds.$$

Since w(t) is the testing-effort spent at time t, W(t) is then the total amount of testing-effort spent in the time interval [0,t).

The failure intensity function or ROCOF of this general testing-effort dependent NHPP model can then be obtained as

$$\lambda(t) = \frac{dm(t)}{dt} = arw(t)e^{-rW(t)}.$$

This model is thus a direct generalization of the GO-model and it reduces to the GO-model when W(t) is a linear function of t. By using different testing-effort functions, i.e. by taking different functions for w(t) and by integrating them with respect to t, different NHPP models suitable in different situations can be obtained.

Usually, the time-dependent behaviour of development effort in the software development process can be expressed by an exponential or a Rayleigh curve, see Yamada et al. (1986b). Some testing-effort dependent reliability models based on the assumption that the testing-effort behaviour during software testing is described by the exponential curve or the Rayleigh curve as well as the software development effort, have been studied.

Sometimes the testing-effort expenditure is difficult to be described by only exponential and Rayleigh curves since actual testing-effort data show various expenditure patterns. A Weibull curve as the testing-effort function, which has flexibility to describe a number of testing-effort expenditure patterns is then presented in Yamada and Ohtera (1990). Here, we give a brief presentation of this general formulation.

Generally, the Weibull-type testing-effort function is defined as

$$w(t) = \alpha\beta\gamma t^{\gamma-1}e^{-\beta t^{\gamma}},$$

where the parameters α, β and γ are positive constants. Here, α denotes the total amount of testing-effort required by software testing, β is a scale parameter and γ is a shape parameter.

Note that the exponential testing-effort functions are those with γ=1 and the Rayleigh testing-effort functions have γ=2. Hence, both are special cases of this Weibull testing-effort function.

For the Weibull-type testing-effort function, the total amount of testing-effort spent during [0,t) is then derived as

$$W(t) = \int_0^t w(s)\,ds = \alpha\left(1 - e^{-\beta t^\gamma}\right).$$

Hence, the overall mean value function of this NHPP model is given by

$$m(t) = a\left[1 - exp\left\{-r\alpha(1 - e^{-\beta t^\gamma})\right\}\right].$$

Generally, by using another testing-effort function, we get an NHPP model with another overall mean value function and it gives us another software reliability model. The estimation of the parameters can be carried out by using this mean value function. It is also possible to estimate the parameters in the testing-effort function separately using the method of least squares, see e.g. Ohtera et al. (1990a).

It should be noted here that there is another interpretation of the testing-effort dependent software reliability models, i.e. it can be seen as a time-transformed version of the GO-model. Generally, given W(t) which can be any time-transformation function, the testing-effort dependent model is just a transformation of the GO-model to another testing-effort dependent time scale. That the failure process is an NHPP follows then directly and the analysis can be carried out as for any NHPP model.

4.5.3. Models for multiple-type of faults

One of the serious critiques on many software reliability models is that all software faults are assumed to be of the same size. A direct modification of the existing models is to assume that there are several different types of faults and some faults are easier to detect than others.

Yamada et al. (1985) proposed a software reliability growth model by assuming that there are two types of software faults for which one type of faults is much easier to be detected than another. The model is based on an NHPP model with mean value function

$$m(t) = a_1\left(1 - e^{-b_1 t}\right) + a_2\left(1 - e^{-b_2 t}\right) = \sum_{i=1}^{2} a_i\left(1 - e^{-b_i t}\right),$$

where a_1, a_2, b_1 and b_2 are parameters expressed as

a_1 = the expected number of initial faults belonging to type one,
a_2 = the expected number of initial faults belonging to type two,
b_1 = the fault-detection rate of type one fault,
b_2 = the fault-detection rate of type two fault.

Other useful quantities may also be derived using these parameters, e.g. the total number of initial faults a is given by

$$a = a_1 + a_2,$$

while the proportion of type 1 faults p_1 is

$$p_1 = \frac{a_1}{a_1 + a_2} = \frac{a_1}{a},$$

and similarly, the proportion of type 2 faults p_2 is

$$p_2 = \frac{a_2}{a_1 + a_2} = \frac{a_2}{a}.$$

For this two-type of faults model, the intensity function is calculated as

$$\lambda(t) = \frac{dm(t)}{dt} = \sum_{i=1}^{2} a_i b_i e^{-b_i t} = a \sum_{i=1}^{2} p_i b_i e^{-b_i t}.$$

This two-type of faults model has also been generalized in Kapur and Garg (1990b) by introducing the probability of imperfect debugging. Interested readers are referred to that paper and for other models including an imperfect debugging probability, the paper by Ohba and Mei (1989) is also of interest.

It should be noted here that the two-type of faults model can be treated as a superposed NHPP model. Suppose that we have two different failure processes which are NHPP with mean value functions $m_1(t)$ and $m_2(t)$, respectively. Then the superposed failure process is also NHPP since the superposition of two independent NHPP's is still NHPP with the mean value function given by

$$m(t) = m_1(t) + m_2(t) .$$

If $m_i(t)$, i=1,2, are taken from two different GO-models, then we have the two-type of faults model discussed before. However, $m_i(t)$ can be any other mean value function and the general description is still valid, perhaps more reasonable models can be obtained with other choices. An attempt similar to this can also be found in Kareer et al. (1990).

The two-type of faults model can simply be generalized by assuming that there are k types of faults. The overall mean value function of the superposed NHPP is then the sum of the mean value function of each failure process assumed to be NHPP. However, a large number of parameters are usually involved and it then requires a large amount of data to get accurate estimates of the parameters.

A simplified model for k-type of faults has been proposed by Khoshgoftaar (1988). The NHPP model with mean value function which has a k-stage Erlangian growth curve is used and it is given by

$$m(t) = a\left[1 - e^{-bt} \sum_{j=0}^{k-1} \frac{(bt)^j}{j!} \right].$$

In the above a is the expected number of initial software faults and b is called the fault detection rate per fault in the steady state while k is a power law parameter.

For this model, it can be observed that if k=1, then it reduces to the GO-model and for k=2, it becomes the delayed S-shaped NHPP model. Note also that for this model, the number of parameters is limited to three but the proportion of the number of each type-i faults is restricted.

4.6. Comments on using NHPP models

Among the existing models, NHPP models have been widely applied by practitioners. The theory of NHPP's is well developed and can be found in most of the established literature on stochastic processes. The application of NHPP to reliability analysis has a long history and can be found in elementary literature on reliability. The calculation of the expected number of failures up to time t is very simple due to the existence of mean value function. The estimates of the parameters are easily obtained by using either the method of maximum likelihood or the method of least squares.

There is a need to study the factors which may affect the testing process in order to obtain a good model to describe the software failure process. NHPP models are useful in many different situations, such as for the cases when we have nonhomogeneous testing, changing software, combination of software and hardware failures etc.

Other important advantages of NHPP models which should be stressed here are that NHPP's are closed under superposition and time-transformation. If we have several failure processes, which can be useful to describe different types of software failures, for example in case of both software or hardware failures, failures of different parts of the system, etc., then the superposed failure process, that is the sum of the failure processes is still NHPP provided that the underlying processes are independent. In this case, we can easily incorporate two or more existing NHPP models by summing up the corresponding mean value functions. The failure intensity of the superposed process is also just the sum of the failure intensity of the underlying processes.

The properties that NHPP is closed under superposition and time-transformation are very interesting and important. However, such properties have not been directly considered in software reliability studies although there are some existing software reliability models such as the testing-effort dependent models and the two-type of faults models for which similar ideas have been adopted. Thus, there is a great research potential here.

NHPP models are useful to describe reliability growth and they have been studied in hardware reliability analysis. Generally, we may use NHPP models in studying software reliability growth as well. By using different mean value functions, we can fit software failure data to some satisfactory degree. However, it depends on how many parameters we have in our model. More parameters are better from a goodness-of-fit point of view, but the computational effort will increase and the confidence of the estimates will be weaker.

However, it should be stressed here that NHPP models are originally introduced for the analysis of hardware failure data and the applicability to pure software system may be questioned. The failure intensity for any pure software systems is discontinuous. This is an obvious difference between hardware and software which is not used for NHPP models.

There is a lack of arguments which are theoretically sound, to use too complicated NHPP models. The GO-model is simple and it can usually be used to get some indication of the rate of reliability growth. The S-shaped software reliability growth models can sometimes be used when there is a strong evidence of the S-shapedness. However, it is more important in practice to use sequential approach by re-estimation of the parameters when we collect more data.

The Musa's basic execution time model is a commonly accepted one when talking about execution time. Many other models can directly be adapted using execution time. It should be noted here that NHPP models are capable of coping with the case of nonhomogeneous testing and hence it is useful for calendar time data as well as for execution time data.

4.7. Bibliographic notes

There are many interesting papers on NHPP modelling of software failure processes. General treatment of NHPP software reliability growth models can be found in the papers by Goel (1980a), (1985), Yamada and Osaki (1983a), (1985a), (1985c) and Musa (1984).

Some interesting original papers presenting NHPP models discussed in this chapter are: Schneidewind (1975), Musa (1975), Goel and Okumoto (1979), Ohba et al. (1982), Musa and Okumoto (1984b), Littlewood (1984), Yamada and Osaki (1983b), (1985b), Schagen and Sallih (1987) and Kapur and Garg (1990b).

The execution time theory leading to the Musa model discussed in Section 4.4 has been extensively treated in the book by Musa et al. (1987a). Some related models are presented in Musa (1975), (1979b), Musa and Okumoto (1984b). See also the papers by Musa (1979b), Musa and Okumoto (1984a), (1986) and Govil (1984).

S-shaped NHPP models have been studied in Ohba et al. (1982), Ohba and Yamada (1984), Yamada and Osaki (1983b), Yamada et al. (1983), (1984c), Ohba et al. (1984), Schagen (1987), Uemero et al. (1990), Kapur and Garg (1990b), (1991b), Adams (1991) and Vallee and Ragot (1991).

Other papers discussing NHPP models are Strandberg and Andersson (1982), Musa (1984), Musa and Okumoto (1984a), Goel (1985), Yamada and Osaki (1985a), Yamada et al. (1985), (1986b), (1986c), Kitaoka et al. (1986), Noon (1986), Ohba and Chou (1989), Yamada and Ohtera (1990), Ohtera et al. (1990c), Jones (1991) and Knafl and Sacks (1991).

Estimation of the parameters in NHPP models is discussed in Schneidewind (1975), Goel and Okumoto (1979), Goel (1980a), Strandberg and Andersson (1982), Yamada and Osaki (1983b), Ehrlich and Emerson (1987), Khoshgoftaar (1988), Vallarino (1989) and Joe (1989).

5

Some Static Models

Time is an essential element in the models such as Markov models and NHPP models which are useful to describe the entire failure process. Hence, these models can be treated as dynamic ones. In this chapter, we present some existing software reliability models for which no dynamic assumption about the software failure process is involved. Time is not an important variable in such models which here includes input-domain-based models, fault-seeding models and software metrics models. Note that unlike other models discussed in the previous chapters, this class of models is mainly useful for the estimation of the number of software faults and it is usually assumed that faults are not removed immediately after detection. These models will only be discussed briefly in the following sections. We also present some other models for the estimation of the number of software faults and provide some references related to the models discussed here.

5.1. Input-domain related software reliability models

It is sometimes important, especially for mission software, to know the probability of a successful execution of the software. Denote by X a variable indicating the outcome of an execution and let

$$X = \begin{cases} 1, & \textit{if the execution is successful}; \\ 0, & \textit{otherwise}. \end{cases}$$

Let p be the failure probability of a test run, that is p=P[X=0]. Then the reliability can be defined as the probability of success of the test run, which is equal to

$$R = 1 - p = P[X=1].$$

An input-domain related model considers the software input space from which test cases are chosen and the studied quantity is the probability that a randomly chosen input datum according to the operational profile, will lead to a failure. By recording the output results from a series of test cases, this probability can be estimated using some statistical sampling techniques.

5.1.1. The Nelson model

A method for estimating software reliability has been presented in Nelson (1978) based on the results of test runs. It is assumed that a number of test cases are chosen from the "operational profile" of the software and after having observed n^* failures among n runs, the reliability may then be estimated by

$$\hat{R} = 1 - \frac{n^*}{n}, \quad n^* \leq n.$$

Note that n*/n is just the estimated probability of the failure of a test run. This simple procedure does not require any other information of the software than the outcome of the test runs.

An intuitive definition of software reliability is the probability that no failures occur during the execution. If a set of infinite test runs is taken, then the limit is the reliability defined as

$$R = \lim_{n \to \infty} \left(1 - \frac{n^*}{n}\right), \quad n^* \leq n,$$

where n is the number of runs and n^* is the number of failures among these n runs.

This is the theoretical definition of the software reliability on which the Nelson model is based. It is in fact a discrete counterpart of the time-dependent definition of software reliability. When the number of data tested is time-dependent, that is, if n is a function of time, the number of failures, n^*, is also time-dependent and we have then a time-dependent definition of the reliability.

The statistical basis for software reliability assessment using the Nelson model is the following. Assume that the input space of the software, E, is divided into M subsets, that is

$$E = \{E_1, E_2, \dots, E_M; M > 0\}.$$

The reliability of a single execution of the software, R_1, is then equal to

$$R_1 = \sum_{i=1}^{M} p_i X_i,$$

where p_i is the probability of choosing an input datum from E_i and

$$X_i = \begin{cases} 1, & \textit{if input } E_i \textit{ leads to correct output;} \\ 0, & \textit{otherwise.} \end{cases}$$

The quantity $\{p_i; i=1,2,\dots,M\}$ is called the operational profile of the software which describes the user condition and it is assumed to be known completely.

If each test run consists of n executions of the software, then the reliability of the test run is

$$R(n) = \prod_{j=1}^{n} R_j = exp\left\{ \sum_{j=1}^{n} ln R_j \right\}.$$

A drawback of the Nelson model and other input-domain-based models is that a large amount of testing is necessary in order to get highly accurate estimate of the reliability. However, it can be shown that under some general conditions, the estimate of reliability according to the Nelson model is an unbiased estimate of the operational reliability.

It is essential that the probability of choosing a certain input datum for testing is equal to the corresponding probability in the operational condition specified by the operational profile, p_i. It can be the case that test data are not representative of the operational profile so this model will give a biased estimate of the reliability.

In order to run the test according to the operational condition, we have to know the operational profile. In general, this is not possible since M, although finite for all programs having finite number of input variables each of which has a finite range, can be very large. Hence, the set of $\{p_i, i=1,2,...M\}$ cannot be obtained accurately and further assumptions have to be made.

In an attempt to solve some of these problems, Brown and Lipow (1975) proposed a modified version of the Nelson model. The input space E is divided into r subspaces, E_1, E_2, ..., and E_r. Assume that the sets E_i, i=1,...,r, are disjoint which is the case when the software does not contain many faults. The failure probability of each subspace is estimated by the outcome of the test runs. The estimation of the reliability can then be carried out using the basic statistical theory for a stratified sampling.

Suppose that n_i is the number of test cases taken from input subspace E_i, i=1,2,...,r. Denote by f_i the number of failures out of n_i runs. The reliability can then be estimated by

$$\widehat{R} = 1 - \sum_{i=1}^{r} \frac{f_i}{n_i} p(E_i),$$

where $\{p(E_i), i=1,2,...,r\}$ is the set of probability measures describing the operational profile of the software, that is $p(E_i)$ is the probability that the input datum is taken from the subspace E_i in usage.

Note that in the above equation, f_i/n_i is just an estimate of the failure probability of a randomly chosen datum from subspace E_i. The sum is thus an estimate of the unreliability of the software.

5.1.2. Some input-domain-based models

Each software has its specified input space and an input space is defined as the set of data which can be used as input to the software. Usually, some input data will give incorrect output while others will not. An input domain-based model specifies the input space and studies the probability that an input datum leads to a failure.

The Nelson model discussed above can be treated as a special case of the input-domain-based models. Some input-domain-based models have been discussed by Bastani and Ramamoorthy (1986). Also in Weiss and Weyuker (1988) a general formulation is presented. However, all of these models have been developed from a theoretical point of view and focus on the correctness of the program. Here, we just outline some basic ideas.

Denote by **I** the input domain of a program **P**. Here, the program **P** is defined as a mapping from the input domain **I** into an output space **O**. The size of a fault is defined as the probability that a datum selected from **I** will result in a failure due to the fault. The input-domain-based model uses the concept of probability equivalence class, E, which is a subset of **I**.

For a subset E of **I**, if **P** is correct for all elements in E with probability $P(X_1,...,X_d)$, supposing that **P** is correct for each X_i in E, i=1,...,d, then E is said to be a probability equivalence class. In this case $P(I/X)$ is the correctness probability of program **P** based on the set of test cases X.

The correctness probability of the program using the continuity assumption can be estimated. Bastani and Ramamoorthy (1986) proposed that the probability equivalence classes should be derived from the requirement specification and the program source code in order to minimize control flow errors.

In Bastani and Ramamoorthy (1986) some general advantages and disadvantages of this model have been discussed. Also, they studied a fuzzy-set-based input domain model which has been proposed in order to develop more theoretically sound models.

Weiss and Weyuker (1988) presented some general theories of input-domain-based software reliability modelling. The reliability of a software is generally defined as the correctness of the software and a tolerance function is introduced to characterize an acceptable level of correctness. Together with a given operational input distribution of the input space, the reliability is estimated by incorporating the actual discrepancy between the functional behaviour of the software and its specification together with a tolerance function. Interested readers are referred to the original paper by Weiss and Weyuker (1988) where further theoretical details can be found.

5.1.3. Some other test-run reliability models

There are several other models for estimation of the probability of a correct execution of the software. Such models are usually empirical and relate this probability to the number of tests in a systematic way.

Generally, test run reliability p is a function of test instance i, expressed as p(i). Some simple functions of p(i) are for example linear, inverse linear and exponential. For the linear case

$$p(i) = a + bi \ , a{\geq}0, b{\geq}0 \ .$$

The inverse linear case is expressed as

$$p(i) = p(\infty) - \frac{\alpha}{i}.$$

The exponential case is given by the relation

$$p(i) = ab^i, \ a{\geq}0, b{\geq}0 \ .$$

Generally, empirical data can be fitted and the parameters may then be estimated. Note that if we treat i as a time-dependent variable, then we may modify the input-domain-based models and obtain a dynamic model. In this case, dynamic models and static models can be related to each other.

5.2. Some fault-seeding models

All software failures are due to the existing software faults which are of a discrete nature. A statistical sampling technique called "capture-recapture" sampling can be used to estimate software reliability. It is assumed that a known number of faults, called "seeded" faults, are inserted into the software and during the testing we detect both seeded faults and inherent faults. The number of remaining faults after testing can then be estimated by the observed numbers of both faults.

The best known seeding model is the Mills model which was published originally as an internal report in 1970, see e.g. Schick and Wolverton (1978) and Duran and Wiorkowski (1981).

Denote by M the number of seeded faults. Suppose that during the testing, k faults are detected and m of them are recognized as seeded faults. Hence, the number of inherent faults detected is k-m. If both inherent faults and seeded faults are equally likely detected, then an estimate of the total number of inherent faults is

$$\widehat{N} = \frac{M(k-m)}{m}.$$

Denote by X_k the number of seeded faults among the total number of k detected faults. Denote by p_i the probability of detecting i seeded faults, that is

$$p_i = P(X_k = i | M),$$

then it can be shown that X_i follows the hypergeometric distribution by the results of capture-recapture sampling. Explicitly, the following holds,

$$p_m(N) = \frac{\binom{M}{m}\binom{N}{k-m}}{\binom{N+M}{k}}.$$

It can be shown that the above estimate of the number of inherent faults N is the maximum likelihood estimate which maximizes $p_m(N)$ with respect to N. Also confidence limits for N can easily be determined.

Some drawbacks should be pointed out here. To begin with, it is essential that seeded faults have the same probability to be detected as the inherent faults. This is in practice impossible since it is the probability of detecting the inherent faults that we want to estimate. Hence in practice, seeded faults can hardly be made as representative as the inherent faults and this will make the estimate biased and inaccurate.

Sometimes, when we do have some prior knowledge of the undetected faults, a seeded fault may also "mask" an inherent fault in the sense that it makes the inherent fault undetectable. Knight and Ammann (1985) presented some experimental results where it is observed that a seeded fault may sometimes have corrective effect on an inherent fault. If this occurs, the estimate will also be biased and underestimate the real number of inherent faults.

Another important aspect is that it costs to carry out software testing. Usually, a test team wants to increase the test effectiveness whenever it is possible. But by adding new faults, the test effectiveness is decreased. However, an advantage of this model is that seeding models can be a helpful tool in studying test effectiveness. Some modifications are necessary in order to construct an applicable seeding model.

An alternative approach is that testing is carried out by two different test teams. Faults detected by the first test team can then be used as seeded faults for the second test team. The number of faults detected by the second test team and the number of faults detected by both test teams may then be used to estimate the reliability.

Denote by m_1 the number of detected faults by the first test team. Assume that among m_1 faults, r faults are also detected by the second test team which has detected totally m_2 faults. An estimate of the number of inherent faults is then

$$\widehat{N} = \frac{m_1(m_2 - r)}{r}.$$

In this case the test effectiveness is not as seriously reduced as for the original Mills model. However, it is important that two test teams work independently and all faults are equally likely detected by both test teams. This is the main disadvantage of this model since they usually are able to detect same types of faults.

However, like other static models, seeding models are only useful for estimating the number of remaining faults and they are of limited use since they can not be used prior to the testing phase. Because of these reasons, the study of the seeding models has now almost terminated in software reliability analysis.

5.3. Models using software complexity metrics

It has been observed at the beginning of the seventies, see e.g. Akiyama (1971), that there is a strong dependence between the number of faults and the nature of the program, such as the number of codes, the number of paths and other algorithmic complexity measures. In this section, we discuss some existing empirical models based on different complexity measures of a software. Software metrics have been widely applied in different contexts, mainly during the design stage for which software metrics are helpful tools in allocating development resources and making management decisions. Here we only discuss those complexity measures in connection with software reliability measurement.

5.3.1. Models related to the Halstead metrics

One of the most well-known software complexity metrics is the so-called Halstead metric, also known as the Halstead software science. It has been developed mainly as a measure of software size and other related quantities. Application to software reliability is focused on the prediction of the number of software faults.

It is reasonable to assume that the number of software faults depends on the size and the complexity of the software. The more complex the software is, the more likely that the software will have a large number of faults. The estimate of the number of faults N, using the Halstead metric, is proportional to the volume of the software V,

$$\widehat{N} = \frac{V}{E_0},$$

where E_0 is a constant of proportionality corresponding to the mean time of mental discriminations between lapses measured in units of mental discriminations according to the Halstead software science.

The volume of the software, V, is defined by

$$V = (n_1 \log_2 n_1 + n_2 \log_2 n_2)\log_2(n_1 + n_2),$$

where n_1 and n_2 are the number of unique operators and operands, respectively.

Also the quantity

$$N = n_1 \log_2 n_1 + n_2 \log_2 n_2$$

is called the program length which is similar to the count of executable statements. According to the Halstead software science, V is preferable as a size metric.

The Halstead software science has been studied by various researchers. An empirical rule usually referred to is that E_0 can be set to 3000. Depending on human unreliability, other values instead of 3000 can be used. Some authors have shown satisfactory results using this rule while others disagree with this empirical formula.

There is certainly a correlation between the number of faults and the Halstead metrics, but the dependence is not necessarily linear. Even if the dependence is linear, the constant of proportionality needs not be equal to $1/E_0$. However, the linearity is a first order approximation.

The model also suffers from many other critiques like other complexity metrics models in software reliability analysis, see e.g. Section 5.3.3. Because the number of software faults is subjected to random influence, the evidence to use very complex formula can not be justified.

5.3.2. Some other software metrics models

There are many other software complexity metrics proposed in the literature. Most of them are strongly correlated to the number of detectable software faults. Hence, they can be used in estimating the fault content of the software. The number of lines of instructions is the simplest one of software complexity metrics which has been studied by many authors. Another interesting measure of software complexity is the number of executable codes in the software.

These metrics can be classified as software size metrics which measure the size of the software. Other software metrics related to software reliability are for example structure metrics such as characteristics of module connections, understandablility metrics and psychological metrics during the software development. There are many other factors which affect the development of software and their reliability.

Below, we present some existing models for estimating the number of faults using some of other software complexity metrics. There are many empirical results from existing literature. Note that most of the relations between the number of software faults and other complexity metrics are usually company-dependent and there are many other factors affecting this, see Section 5.3.3 for some general discussions.

Denote the number of executable codes by S, then the number of faults can for example, be estimated by

$$\widehat{N} = \left(a_1 + a_2 \ln S + a_3 \ln^2 S\right) S,$$

where a_1, a_2 and a_3 are parameters to be determined by using previous software data, see Lipow (1982).

Another empirical formula for estimating the number of faults by Lipow (1982) suggests that

$$\widehat{N} = a + bS^c,$$

where as before parameters a, b and c are to be determined using empirical data. The basis for use of c=4/3 has been presented by Gaffney (1984). Note that an empirical linear regression line has been used as early as in 1971 by Akiyama (1971).

The Halstead model has been modified in Schneider (1981) where the following empirical equation is used

$$\widehat{N} = 7.6 E^{2/3} S^{1/3},$$

where E is the overall reported professional effort in man-months and S is the overall count of thousands of coded source statements of software. A further relation between the number of faults and the number of subprograms, n, is suggested as

$$\widehat{N} = n^{2/3}\left(\frac{S}{.047}\right)^{5/3}.$$

There are many more empirical results presented in the existing literature and the study of software metrics is an active field of software engineering. Due to the importance of the software faults and their impact on software development, the relation between the number of software faults and other software metrics has to be studied.

However, the relation is usually company-dependent and there are also more than just one metric which will affect the number of software faults. This is indicated in Lennselius et al. (1987) and further discussion can be found in Lennselius and Rydström (1990).

5.3.3. Notes on software complexity models

Software complexity measures which are widely used by software engineers in studying software development process are useful for the estimation of the number of existing faults. Such methods have been studied in the early seventies, see e.g. Akiyama (1971) where the number of faults is demonstrated to be strongly correlated to the number of program steps, the number of decision symbols in the flowchart and the number of subroutine calls. Therefore, the number of software faults can be estimated based on these measures.

The main advantage of using software metrics is just its applicability at earlier stages of the software development. This is of vital importance since it is helpful for software managers to allocate software testing effort, to decide a preliminary release time and to set up the price of the software product. Empirical software metrics models are also very simple and they can easily be calculated.

It should be noted that software metrics can only be used to make an overall estimation of software fault content before the testing starts. After the testing a number of faults are removed and it is important to be able to estimate the number of remaining faults. There are few metrics for making such estimation and this is a problem when using software metrics in estimating software reliability for which the prediction of the future behaviour is more important.

It can happen that the parameters are estimated based on the data set that may not be representative for a wide range of software. Parameters are for example strongly company-dependent. Using complexity metrics in estimating the number of faults may yield very wide confidence intervals which are often not useful.

Most existing software metrics, due to their static nature, do not consider the growth of software reliability. A disadvantage of the existing software metrics models is thus that they give only an estimate of the software fault content which is not equal to the probability of software failure, because different faults may have different occurrence rate. An important area of further research is just the relation between the failure intensity of the software and other software metrics or environmental factors which can be used to connect existing static models to other dynamic models. It should be noted that some statistical techniques discussed in the next chapter are capable to incorporate several different software metrics that affect the reliability of software.

Existing studies have been concentrated on finding a single metric to give an acceptable estimate of the number of faults. However, this may not be successful and it can be the case that more than one metrics will have some impact on the reliability. A better way to utilize several metrics is to combine them using techniques such as multiple-regression analysis, see e.g. Khoshgoftaar and Munson (1990a).

The general conclusion is that software complexity measures are useful in estimating the number of software fault content, especially at an earlier stage of software development which is important from a management point of view. The estimate is usually inaccurate and hence it should be revised as more data have been collected. Also, it is important to combine this estimate together with other dynamic models. In Chapter 7 we will discuss some general regression models which may be used to incorporate software metrics in dynamic models.

5.4. Some other static models

There are many other models for the estimation of the number of software faults. In this section we briefly review some interesting ones which cannot be classified into other classes.

5.4.1. A hypergeometric distribution model

Tohma et al. (1989a) suggested a model for estimating the number of remaining faults using the hypergeometric distribution. It is based on sampling arguments and assumes that there are a number of software faults in the program and the cumulative number of faults is assumed to be a growing function of the number of test which are carried out.

According to Tohma et al. (1989a) a test is defined as a number of test instances which are couples of input data and output data. It is assumed that a number of faults are experienced by a test instance. Detected faults are not removed between test instances and hence same faults can be experienced at two test instances.

Denote by w(i) the number of faults experienced by test instance t_i. Suppose that there are m initial faults and w(i) detected faults are taken randomly from among these m faults. Also denote by N_i the number of faults newly detected by test instance t_i. The hypergeometric model assumes that the number of newly detected faults N_i follows a hypergeometric distribution, that is

$$P(N_i=n) = \frac{\binom{m-C_{i-1}}{n}\binom{C_{i-1}}{w(i)-n}}{\binom{m}{w(i)}},$$

where C_{i-1} is the cumulative number of faults newly detected by test instances $t_1,t_2,...,t_{i-1}$ defined as

$$C_{i-1} = \sum_{j=1}^{i-1} N_j.$$

Different forms of w(i) can be used and it should be related to other software development factors. For example, the number of software test-workers has been used as a parameter in w(i) by Tohma et al. (1989a).

Since N_i is assumed to be hypergeometrically distributed, it follows that the expected number of newly detected faults by test instance t_i is given by

$$EN_i = \frac{(m - C_{i-1})w(i)}{m}, \quad i>0.$$

The unknown parameter m and unknown coefficients of w(i) can easily be estimated using collected data, although numerical algorithms have been used. Using a segmentation technique and composite estimation, improved models have been proposed in Tohma et al. (1989a). See further papers by Tohma et al. (1989b), (1991) and Jacoby and Tohma (1990) for some recent results on these hypergeometric distribution models.

5.4.2. A fault-spreading model

Software development consists of several phases. It is reasonable to assume that a fault introduced in one phase will be spread to other forthcoming phases. A new interesting model, called fault-spreading reliability model, using the spreading of faults through the software development phases is presented in Wohlin and Körner (1990).

Assume that the development of the software has been divided into a number of phases. Denote by $X_{i,j}$ the number of faults on level i caused by one fault on level j-1 and $Z_{i,j}$ the total number of faults on level j assuming that the fault is introduced on level i. It is also defined that $Z_{i,i}=1$ for all i.

Using these definitions, the mean and variance of the total number of faults on level j assuming that the original fault is introduced on level i can be derived. For details, see Wohlin and Körner (1990).

Given the mean and variance of $X_{i,j}$, the mean and variance of $Z_{i,j}$ are given by

$$EZ_{i,j} = \prod_{k=i+1}^{j} EX_{i,k},$$

$$VZ_{i,j} = \sum_{k=i+1}^{j} VX_{i,k} \left\{ \prod_{n=i+1}^{k-1} EX_{i,n} \prod_{n=k+1}^{j} EX_{i,n}^2 \right\}.$$

As a simple example, suppose that the mean of $X_{i,j}$ is $1/p$ and the variance of $X_{i,j}$ is $(1-p)/p^2$. This is for example the case when $X_{i,j}$ is geometrically distributed with parameter p independent of the current level. Then the mean and variance of $Z_{i,j}$ are given by

$$EZ_{i,j} = p^{1-j},$$

$$VZ_{i,j} = \frac{1 - p^{j-i}}{p^{2(j-i)}},$$

from which it can be observed that in this case the mean depends only on the current level. Also the variance depends only on the difference between the number of levels since the fault is introduced.

It is stated that by taking the appropriate sums, other quantities such as the total number of faults caused by one fault made on level i can be obtained. Different probability distributions for each $X_{i,j}$ may also be used to get more realistic models.

This model has been extended in Wohlin and Körner (1990) to consider cost-effectiveness by incorporating some general cost factors. In order to utilize the potential of the model, it has to be validated and data have to be collected. However, it is a model worthy of further research, for example, by incorporating the fault-removal process.

5.4.3. A fault complexity model

An interesting model by ranking the complexity of different faults has been suggested in Nakagawa and Hanata (1989). It is assumed that faults can be ranked by their complexity and in practice, it is the case that many complex faults are detected in later phases of the software development. With some appropriate measures of the complexity of faults, the number of remaining faults can be estimated by studying the increase of the average fault complexity.

According to Nakagawa and Hanata (1989), fault complexity is assumed to be fault detectability, that is the probability of detecting the fault. It is obvious that the ratio of complex faults to simple faults increases as the test progresses. Using the ratio of the number of complex faults to simple faults and by knowing the number of discovered faults, a method is suggested by Nakagawa and Hanata (1989) for the estimation of the number of remaining faults.

The Ratio by Error Complexity (REC) is defined as the number of faults of each fault complexity class divided by the number of all faults to be classified. The most recent REC is the one obtained from the most recently discovered faults before estimation. Native REC may then be obtained from a total number of faults detected during the life cycle. Then software reliability can be estimated using the most recent REC. The main problem here is the classification of the faults according to their degree of complexity. See Nakagawa and Hanata (1989) for some applications and further discussions.

5.5. Bibliographic notes

The Nelson model is first published in Nelson (1978) where many interesting ideas for the estimating the probability of a correct execution are presented. Several versions of input-domain-based models which can be considered as generalizations of the Nelson model have been suggested in literature. Interested readers are referred to the papers by Bastani and Ramamoorthy (1986), Brown (1987) and Weiss and Weyuker (1988).

The seeding model originally proposed by Mill has been widely discussed although this model has never been published. Some critiques and discussions can be found in Huang (1984), (1985), Duran and Wiorkowski (1981) and Schick and Wolverton (1978). Applications of seeding models have also been reported by Knight and Ammann (1985), Ohba (1987) and Arlat et al. (1990b).

There are many interesting papers on software complexity metrics and their applications, for example Ottenstein (1979), Nathan (1979), Bailey and Dingee (1981), Lipow (1982), Davis and LeBlanc (1988), Khoshgoftaar and Munson (1990) and Munson and Khoshgoftaar (1990a), (1989b), (1991). A review of software metrics can be found in Hamer (1986) and Coté et al. (1988).

Software metrics have been widely studied in software engineering literature and some interesting books are

Fenton, N.E. (1991). *Software Metrics - A Rigorous Approach*. Chapman & Hall, London.

Halstead, M.H. (1977). *Elements of Software Science*. North-Holland, Amsterdam.

Kitchenham, B.A. and Littlewood, B. (1989). *Measurement for Software Control and Assurance*. Elsevier, London.

Shooman, M.L. (1983). *Software Engineering*. McGraw-Hill, New York.

Other papers of interest are Nakagawa and Hanata (1989), Wohlin and Körner (1990), Tohma et al. (1989a), (1989b), (1991) and Jacoby and Tohma (1990). The essential results are outlined in Section 5.4.

6

Bayesian Analysis and Modelling

In this chapter we study Bayesian formulations of some existing software reliability models. The Littlewood-Verrall model which is the most widely referred Bayesian model in the existing literature is first presented after a brief introduction to Bayesian analysis. Then some representative Bayesian formulations of the Jelinski-Moranda model are discussed. Finally, other existing Bayesian models and techniques for software reliability analysis are reviewed. Some general comments and literature notes are given at the end of this chapter.

6.1. Introduction to Bayesian software reliability models

One of the difficulties in using the existing Markov and NHPP models is that the parameter estimation is not an easy task. Although methods such as maximum likelihood estimation or least squares estimation can directly be applied and the statistical analysis is straightforward, they sometimes do not give adequate results.

The estimates can be very unstable and sometimes unreasonable, see e.g. Section 3.2.3 for a discussion concerning the maximum likelihood estimation of the parameters of the JM-model. The main reason for the problems such as an infinite number of estimated software faults is that the value of the likelihood function changes just slightly during a long interval of the parameter domain. Also, the dependence between the number of faults and the failure intensity per fault makes it difficult to distinguish between these parameters.

Another drawback of classical estimation techniques is that experiences from similar software and previous information about the software development, which should be combined with the available failure data in order to make more accurate estimation and prediction, cannot be utilized in a systematic manner. Because software systems usually have many similarities and we usually have some information about previous software, it is a waste not to use them.

Attempts have been made in using Bayesian techniques to deal with these problems. Many Bayesian models have been proposed for the analysis of software failure data combined with previous knowledge in form of a so-called prior distribution of the unknown parameter.

For any model of the software failure process, there are a number of parameters to be estimated using collected failure data. Denote these parameters by a parameter vector θ and the entire parameter space is denoted by Ω. Usually, some information about θ is available from earlier experience and failure data of similar software and such information can often be described as prior distribution of θ.

Suppose that the prior density of θ is given by $g(\theta)$. Given a set of test data, $\tilde{t} = \{t_1, t_2, ..., t_n; n > 0\}$, we then have, by the Bayes theorem, that the posterior density of θ given $\tilde{t}$ is

$$h(\theta | \tilde{t}) = \frac{f(\tilde{t} | \theta) g(\theta)}{\int_{\Omega} f(\tilde{t} | \theta) g(\theta) d\theta}, \ \theta \in \Omega,$$

where $f(\tilde{t} | \theta)$ is called the likelihood of the data set $\tilde{t}$ given θ.

Denote by $\hat{\theta}$ an estimate of θ and let $l(\hat{\theta}, \theta)$ be the so-called loss function which is a measure of the importance of the estimation error. The estimation of parameter θ using the Bayesian methods can be carried out by minimizing the expected loss function with respect to the posterior distribution. The estimate is called a Bayes estimate.

Hence, the Bayes estimate of θ can be found by minimizing the so-called posterior expected loss which is given by

$$E\left[l(\hat{\theta}, \theta) | \tilde{t} \right] = \int_{\Omega} l(\hat{\theta}, \theta) h(\theta | \tilde{t}) d\theta, \ \theta \in \Omega.$$

Usually, the loss function is assumed to be quadratic since it is a good approximation of all reasonable loss functions, at least around the true value of θ. The quadratic loss function has the form

$$l(\widehat{\theta},\theta) = c\left(\widehat{\theta} - \theta\right)^2,$$

where c is a constant of proportionality. If the above quadratic loss function is used, we simply get that

$$\widehat{\theta} = E(\theta|\tilde{t}) = \int_\Omega \theta h(\theta|\tilde{t})d\theta,$$

i.e. the Bayes estimate of θ minimizing a quadratic loss is just the mean of the posterior distribution of θ given $\tilde{t}$.

Another interesting loss function which is sometimes used is

$$l(\widehat{\theta},\theta) = c\left|\widehat{\theta} - \theta\right|,$$

and it can be shown that the estimate obtained by minimizing this expected loss is the median of the posterior density function.

Usually, it is difficult to obtain an analytical form of the posterior distribution and numerical algorithms have to be used for a multiple integration. There are, however, some distributions having some appropriate properties which have been widely used in Bayesian analysis. To name a few, uniform distribution, Gamma distribution and Beta distribution are some of them.

In fact, we could take any existing software reliability model and specify any prior distribution for each model parameter to get a new Bayesian model. However, we can generally not get a closed formula for the posterior distribution and multiple integration is often involved. Generally, some further assumptions have to be made for the sake of mathematical tractability.

6.2. The Littlewood-Verrall (LV) model

The model suggested by Littlewood and Verrall (1973) is perhaps the most well-known Bayesian model. The LV-model assumes that times between failures are exponentially distributed with a parameter that is treated as a random variable, which is assumed to have a Gamma prior distribution. The exponentiality is natural and justified by the random testing condition. The choice of Gamma distributed prior is mainly due to its flexibility and mathematical tractability.

Specifically, the successive times between failures, t_i, i=1,2,...,n, are assumed to be independent, exponentially distributed random variables with density function

$$f(t_i|\lambda_i) = \lambda_i exp\{-\lambda_i t_i\}, \quad i=1,2,...,n;$$

where λ_i is an unknown parameter whose uncertainty is due to the randomness of the testing and the random location of the software faults. The uncertainty of λ_i is described by a Gamma distribution with parameter α and $\psi(i)$, that is

$$f(\lambda_i|\alpha,\psi(i)) = \frac{[\psi(i)]^\alpha \lambda_i^{\alpha-1} exp\{-\psi(i)\lambda_i\}}{\Gamma(\alpha)},$$

where α is the shape parameter and $\psi(i)$ is the scale parameter depending on the number of detected faults. By taking different forms for $\psi(i)$, different test environments may be described.

Usually, $\psi(i)$ describes the quality of the test and it is a monotonically increasing function of i. This condition implies that λ_i is stochastically decreasing in i, i.e.

$$P(\lambda_i \le \lambda) \ge P(\lambda_{i-1} \le \lambda), \quad for \ all \ i \ge 1.$$

The likelihood function of t_i, given α and $\psi(i)$, can be derived as the following

$$f(t_i | \alpha, \psi(i)) = \int_0^\infty f(t_i | \lambda_i) g(\lambda_i | \alpha, \psi(i)) d\lambda_i$$

$$= \int_0^\infty \lambda_i \, exp\{-\lambda_i t_i\} \frac{[\psi(i)]^\alpha \lambda_i^{\alpha-1} exp\{-\psi(i)\lambda_i\}}{\Gamma(\alpha)} d\lambda_i$$

$$= \frac{\alpha[\psi(i)]^\alpha}{[t_i + \psi(i)]^{\alpha+1}}.$$

The posterior distribution of t_i, given α and $\psi(i)$, is then given by

$$F(t_i | \alpha, \psi(i)) = 1 - \left[\frac{\psi(i)}{t_i + \psi(i)} \right]^\alpha.$$

It follows that the posterior failure rate function, given α and $\psi(i)$, is simply expressed by

$$\lambda(t_i | \alpha, \psi(i)) = \frac{\alpha}{t_i + \psi(i)}.$$

It can now be noted that for the LV-model, times between failures have a Pareto distribution. Note also that times between failures have a strictly decreasing failure rate, see Figure 6.1, and this can be compared with the JM-model for which we have a constant failure rate due to the exponentiality of the distribution of time between failures.

The likelihood function of the data set $\{t_1, t_2, ..., t_n; n > 0\}$ is then given by,

$$f(t_1, ..., t_n | \alpha, \psi(\cdot)) = \frac{\alpha^n \prod_{i=1}^n [\psi(i)]^\alpha}{\prod_{i=1}^n [t_i + \psi(i)]^{\alpha+1}}.$$

The original estimation of the model parameters proposed by Littlewood and Verrall (1973), that is the parameters in $\psi(i)$ and the parameter α, is carried out by maximizing this joint density function. Due to this reason, this model has been called a parametric empirical Bayesian model by

Mazzuchi and Soyer (1988) where a Bayes empirical-Bayes version of this model is also presented.

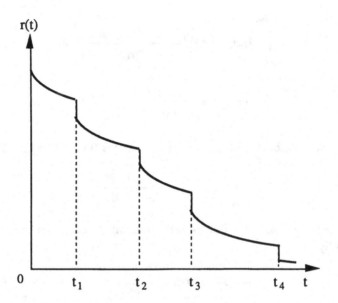

Figure 6.1. The failure intensity curve for the LV-model.

In order to maximize the above joint density function, we need to specify the analytical form of the function $\psi(i)$. As pointed out before, $\psi(i)$ should be an increasing function of i and this ensures that $\lambda(i)$ is stochastically decreasing in i. There are, however, many different choices here depending on different situations.

As an example we may specify $\psi(i)$ to be a linear function of i, that is

$$\psi(i) = \beta_0 + \beta_1 i,$$

which is also originally proposed by Littlewood and Verrall (1973). In the above, β_0 and β_1 are model parameters to be determined.

For this linear case the equations for the determination of the parameters are the following

$$n + \sum_{i=1}^{n} \alpha \left[ln(\beta_0 + \beta_1 i) - ln(t_i + \beta_0 + \beta_1 i) \right] = 0,$$

$$\sum_{i=1}^{n} \left[\frac{\alpha}{\beta_0 + \beta_1 i} - \frac{\alpha + 1}{t_i + \beta_0 + \beta_1 i} \right] = 0,$$

$$\sum_{i=1}^{n} \left[\frac{\alpha i}{\beta_0 + \beta_1 i} - \frac{(\alpha + 1) i}{t_i + \beta_0 + \beta_1 i} \right] = 0.$$

After having estimated $\psi(i)$ and α, we may estimate the current reliability of the software by

$$\widehat{R}(t) = 1 - \widehat{F}(t) = \left[\frac{\widehat{\psi}(i)}{t_i + \widehat{\psi}(i)} \right]^{\widehat{\alpha}}.$$

The Bayes empirical-Bayes model proposed by Mazzuchi and Soyer (1988) assumes that the parameters α, β_1 and β_2 are random variables and appropriate prior distributions are assigned to these parameters. However, due to the computational complexity, some simplifications are necessary. In the paper by Mazzuchi and Soyer (1988), an approximation procedure is used to obtain some computable results. Here, we refer the interested readers to the original paper.

Similar equations can be derived using other functions for $\psi(i)$ and a quadratic form of this function is suggested in Littlewood and Verrall (1973). For the quadratic function, we have

$$\psi(i) = \beta_0 + \beta_1 i^2.$$

Another possibility is to use an exponential-type function, that is

$$\psi(i) = exp\{\beta_0 + \beta_1 i\}.$$

A rational function for $\psi(i)$ has been proposed by Musa (1984). It is based on the idea that the parameter should be inversely related to the number of remaining faults in the software. The relation is suggested to be given by the following function

$$\psi(i) = \frac{N_0 T_0 \alpha}{N_0 - i}.$$

In the above equation, N_0 denotes the expected number of faults during the maintained life of the software, T_0 is the initial mean time to failure and α is the scale parameter of the Gamma distribution as before.

An advantage of using this function for $\psi(i)$ is that it is capable of dealing with the case when we have a finite number of software faults which is given by the parameter N_0.

A model similar to the LV-model has been proposed in Keiller et al. (1983). It is also assumed that the successive failure rates are random variables with Gamma prior distributions. A function describing the reliability growth due to the removing of faults is, however, involved in the shape parameter. That is, the prior distribution of $\lambda(i)$ is then given by

$$f(\lambda_i | \beta, \psi(i)) = \frac{\beta^{\psi(i)} \lambda_i^{\psi(i)-1} exp\{-\beta\lambda_i\}}{\Gamma(\psi(i))}.$$

6.3. Some Bayesian formulations of the JM-model

Because the JM-model is one of the most well-known software reliability models and there are some problems with the maximum likelihood estimates of the model parameters, Bayesian formulations of the JM-model have been studied by various authors. For a discussion of the JM-model, see Section 3.2. By adopting a Bayesian approach, some interesting formulations can be obtained. The Bayesian inference of N_0, the number of initial faults, and ϕ, the failure intensity per fault, can easily be carried out by assigning appropriate prior distributions to them. In this section, we first introduce the general Bayesian formulation of the JM-model by

Langberg and Singpurwalla (1985) together with some modifications. Then other Bayesian formulations based on the JM-model are briefly reviewed.

6.3.1. The Langberg-Singpurwalla model and modifications

Langberg and Singpurwalla (1985) presented a shock model interpretation of software failure and a justification of the JM-model is made. An interesting unification of several existing models is presented. Also some Bayesian models are proposed.

In the Langberg-Singpurwalla Bayesian model the parameters in the JM-model are treated as random variables. Let Φ denote the failure intensity per fault and N the number of faults initially in the software, both being random variable. Given Φ and N, the times between failures are exponentially distributed with parameters Φ and N, that is

$$P(T_i > t_i | N, \Phi) = exp\{-\Phi(N-i+1)t_i\}, \ i \geq 1;$$

and we can assign a prior distribution to the pair (N, Φ). The resultant posterior distribution may be obtained by the Bayes theorem.

In the original paper by Langberg and Singpurwalla (1985), three cases by assigning different prior distributions to the parameters Φ and N are considered. The most general model which includes the other two as special or limiting cases is the following.

Due to the discrete nature of the parameter N, the prior distribution for N is allowed to be any specified discrete distribution given by

$$\pi_k = P(N=k), \ k=0,1,2,\dots;$$

and Φ is assumed to have a Gamma prior distribution with scale parameter a and shape parameter b, i.e.

$$p(\phi) = \frac{a^b \phi^{b-1} e^{-a\phi}}{\Gamma(b)}, \ \phi \geq 0.$$

In this case, the joint posterior distribution of N and Φ given the data set $\tilde{t}=\{t_1,t_2,...,t_n; n>0\}$ is the following

$$P(N=k,\Phi=\phi|\tilde{t}) = \frac{\phi^{b+n-1}exp\{-\phi(a+T_{n,k})\}}{C}\pi_k, \quad k \geq n,$$

where C is a normalizing constant given by

$$C = \Gamma(b+n)\sum_{j=n}^{\infty}\frac{j!}{(j-n)!}(a+T_{n,j})^{-b-n}\pi_j$$

and $T_{n,k}$ is the total time on test defined by

$$T_{n,k} = \sum_{i=1}^{n}(k-i+1)t_i, \quad k \geq n.$$

The posterior probability of Φ given N=k is also Gamma distributed, Gamma (a',b'), with revised shape and scale parameters a' and b' which are given by

$$a' = a+T_{n,k}, \quad b' = b+n,$$

respectively. The posterior marginal probability of N, is

$$P(N=k|\tilde{t}) = \frac{\frac{k!}{(k-n)!}(a+T_{n,k})^{-b-n}\pi_k}{\sum_{j=n}^{\infty}\frac{j!}{(j-n)!}(a+T_{n,j})^{-b-n}\pi_j}, \quad k \geq n.$$

Since N is a discrete (integer) variable, the computation of this posterior distribution is straightforward and can be obtained numerically through a suitable truncation. The Bayesian estimate of N minimizing the quadratic loss function can then be computed as follows

$$\hat{N} = \sum_{k=n}^{\infty}kP(N=k|\tilde{t}).$$

As a simple special case of the above we may assume that N is degenerated at a known value k_0 and Φ has a Gamma prior distribution, in this case the likelihood of ϕ for $k_0 \geq n$ is

$$L(\phi|\tilde{t}) \propto \phi^n exp\left\{-\phi T_{n,k_0}\right\}$$

and it can be shown that the joint density function of $\tilde{t}$, is a multivariate Pareto, see e.g. Langberg and Singpurwalla (1985). In this case, the posterior density of Φ is Gamma distributed with scale parameter a' and shape parameter b'.

An interesting case is when Φ is degenerated at a known value ϕ and N is Poisson. If N is random with a Poisson(λ) prior distribution and Φ is known to be equal to ϕ, then we have similarly as before that

$$L(N=k|\tilde{t}) \propto \frac{k!}{(k-n)!}\phi^n exp\left\{-\phi T_{n,k}\right\}, \ k \geq n,$$

and by using Bayes theorem, it can be shown, see e.g. Langberg and Singpurwalla (1985), that the posterior probability is

$$P(N=k|\tilde{t}) = \frac{\left[\lambda e^{-\phi \Sigma_{i=1}^n t_i}\right]^{k-n}}{(k-n)!} exp\left\{-\lambda e^{-\phi \Sigma_{i=1}^n t_i}\right\}, \ k \geq n.$$

Hence, it follows that the posterior distribution of (N-n) is Poisson with mean

$$\gamma(t_1,t_2,...,t_n) = \lambda exp\left\{-\phi \sum_{i=1}^n t_i\right\}.$$

6.3.2. Other Bayesian formulations of the JM-model

There are several other Bayesian formulations of the JM-model proposed by various authors. Below we briefly outline some existing results of general interests.

Jewell (1985) presented a further Bayesian formulation of the JM-model following that of Langberg and Singpurwalla (1985). As for the Langberg-Singpurwalla Bayesian model the parameter Φ is assumed to be Gamma a priori and the number of initial software faults N is assumed to be a random variable having a Poisson(Λ) distribution. The difference between the Jewell´s formulation and that of Langberg and Singpurwalla is that Λ is further assumed to have a Gamma prior distribution.

In this case, N is unknown with Poisson(λ) prior distribution, and given λ and ϕ, the likelihood of the data $\tilde{t}$ is

$$L(\tilde{t}|\lambda,\phi) = \frac{(\lambda\phi)^n e^{-\phi T_{n,n}} exp\{-\lambda(1-e^{-\phi t})\}}{n!}.$$

From the above it can be seen that if $\phi t >> 1$, we have

$$L(\tilde{t}|\lambda,\phi) \propto (\lambda\phi)^n exp\{-\phi T_{n,n} - \lambda\}.$$

Hence, a suitable choice of the prior distribution of λ is Gamma,

$$p(\lambda) = Gamma(\lambda|a,b) = \frac{b^a \lambda^{a-1} e^{-b\lambda}}{\Gamma(a)}.$$

In this case, given the data set $\tilde{t} = \{t_1, t_2, ..., t_n; n > 0\}$, the posterior density $p(\lambda|\tilde{t})$ is also Gamma with the revised parameters a' and b' given by

$$a' = a+n, \ b' = b+1.$$

By assigning Gamma($\Phi|c,d$) to the prior for Φ, it follows that the posterior distribution is still Gamma with the revised parameters

$$c' = c+n, \ d' = d+T_{n,n}.$$

Although the computation of the posterior distributions of the parameters is usually not an easy task, the computation of the predictive distribution for the number of undetected faults, $\overline{N}$, is straightforward. The predictive density is given by, see Jewell (1985),

$$p(\overline{N}|\tilde{t}) = \int \int p(\overline{N}|\lambda, \Phi, \tilde{t}) p(\lambda, \Phi|\tilde{t}) \, d\lambda \, d\Phi$$

$$= K \frac{\Gamma(a'+\overline{N})}{\Gamma(a')\overline{N}(b')^{\overline{N}}} \left(\frac{d'}{d'+\overline{N}t}\right)^{c'}$$

where K is a normalizing constant.

In a paper by Littlewood and Sofer (1987) a reparameterized version of the JM-model in order to avoid the discrete parameter for the initial number of faults is presented. After the reparametrization we get two continuous parameters, the initial program failure intensity and the constant amount failure rate per fault.

Let $\lambda = N\phi$ where λ is the initial failure intensity of the software and ϕ may be interpreted as an improvement factor which is defined as the expected decrease in the failure intensity by removing a software fault. This reparametrization is justified by the fact that even when the likelihood has its maximum at infinity in N, λ is usually finite and positive. By assigning an appropriate prior distribution to (λ, ϕ) and using the collected data set $\tilde{t}$, the posterior distribution can be calculated in the usual manner.

The independent multiplicative Gamma-type priors are used in Littlewood and Sofer (1987), namely,

$$Prior(\lambda, \phi) = Prior(\lambda) Prior(\phi)$$

where $Prior(\lambda)$ and $Prior(\phi)$ are assumed to be Gamma(a,b) and Gamma(c,d), respectively, that is,

$$Prior(\lambda) = \frac{b^a \lambda^{a-1} e^{-b\lambda}}{\Gamma(a)}, \quad \lambda > 0;$$

$$Prior(\phi) = \frac{d^c \phi^{c-1} e^{-d\phi}}{\Gamma(c)}, \quad \phi > 0.$$

Generally, given the data set $\tilde{t}=\{t_1,t_2,...,t_n; \; n>0\}$, the posterior distribution of λ and ϕ can be computed as

$$p(\lambda,\phi|t_1,...,t_n) = Cp(t_1,...,t_n|\lambda,\phi)Prior(\lambda,\phi),$$

where C is a normalizing constant for which

$$\frac{1}{C} = \int\int p(t_1,...,t_n|\lambda,\phi)Prior(\lambda,\phi)d\lambda d\phi.$$

For $\lambda>(n-1)\phi$, the likelihood function of the data set, which is zero otherwise, is given by

$$p(t_1,...,t_n|\lambda,\phi) = \prod_{i=1}^{n}\left[\lambda-(i-1)\phi\right]exp\left\{-\left[\lambda-(i-1)\right]t_i\right\}.$$

Using these results, other reliability measures, such as the current reliability, the current failure rate, etc., can be derived. Also, the predicative distribution for the future reliability and other reliability attributes such as the mean time to next failure, the number of remaining faults are also obtained. Interested readers are referred to the original paper by Littlewood and Sofer (1987).

It is essential to predict the failure intensity, although many models are proposed for the purpose of estimation. Csenki (1990) used the concepts of Bayesian prediction theory in obtaining the predictive distribution of the time to next failure. The underlying assumption is also that of the JM-model. It also assumed that the number of faults is random with a Poisson distribution a priori and the failure intensity per fault has a Gamma distribution a priori.

Under these assumptions, the predictive distribution is obtained and the posterior probability of the software to be fault-free is also given. The original paper by Csenki (1990) contains more theoretical results and interested readers are referred to that paper. However, numerical problems are involved in computing the posterior distribution and other related quantities.

6.4. Other Bayesian software reliability models

In general, we may choose any existing software reliability model and by incorporating any prior distribution, we get a new Bayesian model. However, because finding a closed posterior distribution is not easy, there are few other pure Bayesian models in the existing literature. Hence, this is an area for further research. In this section we give a brief review of some other existing Bayesian software reliability models for the sake of completeness.

6.4.1. A model for fault-free probability

Most of the existing models do not allow for an infinite life time of the software system. Sometimes it is believed that the software is perfect and it contains no further faults. Even though this probability is very low, at least for reasonably large systems, it may cause some problems in practice, since the mean time to next failure may be infinity. Thompson and Chelson (1980) studied a Bayesian reliability model dealing with probability of fault-free software.

Denote by p, $0 \le p \le 1$, the probability that the software is not fault-free, that is, it contains one or more faults. Suppose that given $p>0$ which means that the software does contain further faults, the reliability is exponential with an unknown parameter $\lambda \ge 0$. In this case, the reliability function given λ and p can be expressed as

$$R(t|\lambda,p) = (1-p) + pe^{-\lambda t}.$$

Denote the prior density of parameter λ by $h(\lambda)$ and let the prior density of parameter p be $g(p)$. Generally, determination of the value of p may be the following. After the testing, p is set to unity if one or more faults are detected. Otherwise, the knowledge on p, $g(p)$, is revised.

The likelihood function of the data set $\tilde{t}=\{t_1,t_2,...,t_n; n>0\}$ is

$$f(t|\lambda,p) = \begin{cases} (1-p) + pe^{-\lambda T}, & \text{for } n=0; \\[2mm] p\dfrac{e^{-\lambda T}(\lambda T)^n}{n!}, & \text{for } n>0. \end{cases}$$

In the above equation T is the total amount of time during which the software is tested and n is the number of failures which have occurred during this time interval.

Specifically, we now assume that the prior distribution of λ, $h(\lambda)$, is Gamma with parameters a and b and the prior distribution of p is Beta with parameters c and d, that is

$$g(p) = \frac{\Gamma(c+d+2)}{\Gamma(c+1)\Gamma(d+1)} p^c (1-p)^d, \; c+1, \, d+1 \geq 0.$$

An explanation of the parameters is the following. The parameter b may be treated as the number of faults during a previous testing of length a and the quantity c/(c+d) may be interpreted as the portion of the delivered software containing faults.

Given that the software does contain faults, then p=1, and the posterior distribution of λ is Gamma distributed with the parameters (a+T,b+n+1). In this case, we may also compute the posterior mean and the posterior variance which are equal to (b+n+1)/(a+T) and (b+n+1)/(a+T)², respectively.

The posterior distribution of the reliability at time t is given by

$$f(R(t)|\tilde{t}) = \frac{\left(\dfrac{a+T}{t}\right)^{b+n} (-lnR)^{b+n-1} R^{(a+T)/t-1}}{\Gamma(b+n)}.$$

Thompson and Chelson (1980) considered also a more general reliability model taking the probability of fault-free software into account. The general model is similar to the previous one except that it is assumed that the reliability function is given by

$$R(t|\lambda_i,p_i;i\geq0) = \sum_{i=0}^{\infty} p_i exp(-\lambda_i t).$$

In the above equation, p_i is the probability that there are exactly i faults and λ_i is the failure intensity of the software, given that it contains i faults. The quantities p_i, $i\geq0$, are taken as Poisson probabilities, that is

$$p_i = \frac{N_0^i}{i!} e^{-N_0}.$$

Note that it is assumed that $\lambda_0=0$ and p_0 is the probability that the software is fault-free.

The following interesting case is further discussed in Thompson and Chelson (1980). Assume that the number of initial faults N_0 in the software is a Poisson distributed random variable with mean n_0. We may then rewrite λ_i as $i\phi$, that is the failure intensity is assumed to be proportional to the number of software faults. It can also be noted that this model may be treated as another general Bayesian formulation of the JM-model.

Usually, the relation between the number of remaining faults and the fault-occurrence rate, that is λ_i as a function of i, is difficult to be established. If we assume that $\lambda_i=\lambda$ for all $i>0$, and let

$$p = p_1 + p_2 + \dots ,$$

we get the simplified model discussed in Thompson and Chelson (1980).

6.4.2. Bayesian formulation of an NHPP model

Although there are many NHPP models suggested and applied in software reliability context, few Bayesian extensions of NHPP models are found in the existing literature. A fully Bayesian approach has, however, been considered by Kyparisis and Singpurwalla (1984) using an NHPP model with mean value function

$$m(t) = \left(\frac{t}{\alpha}\right)^{\beta}.$$

This is the Duane reliability growth model discussed in Section 4.5.1 and it is sometimes called a Weibull process model. This model has previously been applied in the analysis of repairable system reliability.

By assigning a prior distribution to the parameter set (α, β) and by using the failure data set $\tilde{t}$, the posterior distribution can be obtained. For the sake of simplicity, we may take α to be uniformly distributed and β is assumed to be Beta distributed. That is, the following a priori distributions of the parameters α and β are used,

$$g(\alpha) = \frac{1}{\alpha_0}, \quad 0 < \alpha \leq \alpha_0 ;$$

$$f(\beta) = \frac{\Gamma(k_1+k_2)(\beta-\beta_1)^{k_1-1}(\beta_2-\beta)^{k_2-1}}{\Gamma(k_1)\Gamma(k_2)(\beta_2-\beta_1)^{k_2+k_2-1}}, \quad 0 \leq \beta_1 < \beta < \beta_2 , \ k_1, k_2 \geq 0.$$

However, the computation of the posterior distribution is not simple and has to be carried out numerically and approximately. Kyparisis and Singpurwalla (1984) provided some results and some details may also be found in Mazzuchi and Singpurwalla (1988).

6.4.3. A Bayesian model using the geometric distribution

A Bayesian method for estimation and prediction of software reliability using a geometric distribution is studied in Liu (1987). It is an attempt to overcome some drawbacks associated with some earlier models.

Assume that the software is tested by using a sequence of test instances, each consisting of a number of test cases. Denoted by R_i the reliability of the software at the i:th debugging instance. Hence, R_i is the probability that a test case in the i:th test instance will cause a failure.

Denote by X_i the number of test cases at the i:th debugging instance at which the first failure occurs. Then X_i is a discrete random variable having a geometric distribution with parameter R_i, that is

$$P(X_i=k) = R_i^{k-1}(1-R_i), \quad k \geq 1.$$

In the paper by Liu (1987), a Beta prior distribution with parameters a and b is assigned to R_1, that is, R_1 has a prior density function given by

$$f(R_1) = \frac{R_1^{a-1}(1 - R_1)^{b-1}}{\beta(a,b)}; \quad a,b \geq 1.$$

It is also pointed out that the case a=b=1 corresponds to a non-informative prior distribution which is desirable when no information is available. The choice of a Beta prior distribution is mainly due to the fact that it constitutes a conjugate family of posterior distributions.

Observations may then be successively incorporated and posterior distribution can be obtained. Assume that x_1, x_2, ... , are the observed test data, since the prior distribution is Beta which is a conjugate prior, the posterior distribution of R_i is also Beta with revised parameter c_i and d_i given by

$$c_i = c_{i-1} + x_i - 1 = \sum_{j=1}^{i} (x_j - 1) + a,$$

$$d_i = d_{i-1} + 1 = b + 1.$$

Other reliability measures can also be obtained. Under the quadratic loss function, the Bayesian estimation of reliability R_i at the i:th debugging instance is given by

$$\widehat{R}_i = E(R|x_1, x_2, \dots, x_i) = \frac{c_i}{c_i + d_i}.$$

Applications to some real data sets may be found in the original paper by Liu (1987).

6.5. Notes on the application of Bayesian models

The most important feature of using a Bayesian model is that prior information can be incorporated into the estimation procedure. Bayesian methods are especially useful in reliability analysis because the increase in reliability is usually achieved by improving a similar product developed previously. For software systems, there is always some available information about the software development and useful information can also be obtained from similar software products, through for example some measures of the software complexity, the fault-removal history during the design phase, etc.

With an appropriate prior, Bayesian inference is quite accurate and gives much better results than other methods, such as the method of maximum likelihood or least squares. Also, Bayesian methods require fewer test data to achieve a high accuracy of estimation. It should be noted that care must be taken in choosing appropriate prior distributions because an improper prior distribution may give very bad results which can even be worse than the maximum likelihood estimates. However, if no information seems to be available, non-informative priors can still be used and they usually give quite adequate results.

However, existing models seem to be monotonic in a sense that simple and mathematically tractable posterior distributions are few in the existing literature. Most of the existing Bayesian models are also strongly related to the JM-model which is the simplest pure software reliability model and it seems to be quite popular among statisticians, see the models discussed in Abdel-Ghaly et al. (1986) and Mazzuchi and Soyer (1988). It is argued that Bayesian estimates of the parameters in the JM-model usually have better behaviours than the maximum likelihood estimates and this is the reason why many such models are studied.

Most existing Bayesian formulations of the JM-model assume in a sense that the failure intensity per fault follows a Gamma distribution and the number of initial faults is Poisson distributed. These assumptions are used mainly due to the analytical simplicity of the posterior distributions. There is a need to search for other suitable a priori distributions in order to describe other a priori information.

A recent paper by Becker and Camarinopoulos (1990) provides some interesting ideas. Given the value of λ, the time to the first failure is exponential with parameter λ. The prior distribution of λ is assumed to belong to the following class

$$f(\lambda) = e^{-b\lambda} \sum_{i=0}^{n} a_i \lambda^j .$$

It can be shown that this class is closed under multiplication and left-shift operation. Hence, it is a class of conjugate priors with some desirable properties. The original model is one which takes the possibility of a correct program into account and can be seen as a generalization of the model by Thompson and Chelson (1980), see Section 6.4.1. Interested readers are referred to the original papers.

Due to the computational complexity, it is important that posterior distributions are not too complicated. There are also some computational procedures developed, see e.g. Mazzuchi and Soyer (1988). However, as for the Langberg-Singpurwalla's general Bayesian model, the modelling procedures are essentially the same.

An important point here is that there are too many models dealing with the number of software faults which is not the most essential measure of software reliability since different faults may contribute a different amount to the software failure probability. More attention should be paid to the reliability function and other measures such as the mean time to next failure and the current failure intensity. However, for many models the computation is straightforward.

Finally, an important advantage of Bayesian techniques is computation of the confidence region which has not received much attention in software reliability analysis. Most existing results are concerned with point estimation of different parameters. Hence, an area where further research is needed is the Bayesian interval estimation, i.e. the highest posterior density region.

6.6. Bibliographic notes

General theory of Bayesian techniques can be found in many elementary texts on Bayesian statistical analysis, e.g. *"Bayesian Reliability Analysis"* by Martz and Waller (1982, Wiley, New York). Below we list some existing papers in which Bayesian models or present Bayesian formulations of software reliability models are discussed.

The earliest paper presenting a Bayesian model is due to Littlewood and Verrall (1973). See also other papers by Professor Littlewood for some further discussions of this model, e.g. Littlewood (1979a), (1980a) and (1980b) where some other modifications may also be found.

Significant steps towards pure Bayesian analysis of software reliability models have been taken by Professor Singpurwalla and his colleagues. Interesting papers are Meinhold and Singpurwalla (1983), Crow and Singpurwalla (1984), Horigome et al. (1984), Barlow and Singpurwalla (1985) and Langberg and Singpurwalla (1985).

There are many papers dealing with Bayesian treatment of the Jelinski-Moranda model. Important papers are e.g. Langberg and Singpurwalla (1985), Jewell (1985), Littlewood and Sofer (1987), Wright and Hazelhurst (1988), Raftery (1988) and Csenki (1990).

Other interesting papers presenting or discussing Bayesian software reliability models are Thompson and Chelson (1980), Musa (1984), Kyparisis and Singpurwalla (1984), Ross (1985a), Abdel-Ghaly et al. (1986), Langberg and Singpurwalla (1986), Jewell (1986), Liu (1987), Mazzuchi and Soyer (1988), Catuneanu and Mihalache (1985), Horigome and Kaise (1990), Becker and Camarinopoulos (1990) and Bunday and Al-Ayoubi (1990).

7

Some Statistical Data Analysis Techniques

The reliability of a software product is usually estimated and predicted by analysing collected failure data. Inferences may be carried out by using standard statistical methods which can be found in different statistical literature. For example, failure times may be treated as a series of quantities and hence time series analysis can be used in describing the behaviour of the software failure data. Also, because we usually have some known variables which affect the reliability of the software, techniques such as exploratory data analysis have a great potential in predicting software reliability. Regression analysis has also been widely used when we have some software complexity metrics which can be used as explanatory variable. Here, we will mainly discuss the application of time series models and proportional hazard models. These models have been studied in the existing literature in software reliability context and some references are provided at the end of this chapter.

7.1. Time series approach

In practice, software failures are observed successively and the failure data can be treated as a time series, hence, time series models are very useful in predicting the failure behaviour of the software failure process. In this section general time series models are discussed. Some special models such as the random coefficient autoregressive process model by Horigome et al. (1985) and a Fourier series model by Crow and Singpurwalla (1984) are briefly reviewed.

7.1.1. Some general time series models

The general idea of time series analysis is to find a pattern through analysing a series of observations of a variable. From the observations, interesting patterns such as trend and cyclic variation can be identified and the information gained can then be used in predicting future behaviours of the series.

Time series analysis is a widely used technique for the analysis of sequential statistical data, and especially, time series models are helpful tools for the prediction of the future value by using the past and present observations. For the reliability analysis of a software, if a failure time depends on the previous times to failures together with some unpredictable noise factors, time series models may then be directly implemented in analysing software failure data.

There are mainly two important advantages of using time series models, see e.g. Dale and Harris (1982). Firstly, no specific assumptions are made about the software failure process. For example, most existing software reliability models assume that detected faults are perfectly removed and otherwise, failure data has to be modified. However, in practice, especially during the software operation phase, a program is usually restarted without correction after a failure due to the delay of corrective action or the unknown location of the fault causing that failure which makes it impossible to correct at once. Time series models are one of the techniques which are capable of incorporating both the case of correction and the case for which we have no correction after a failure.

Secondly, the advantage of using time series models in analysing software failure data is that, since time series analysis is a well-developed statistical technique and many results exist in standard statistical literature, future behaviour of the failure process may easily be predicted once the parameters have been estimated. Prediction is usually a more important subject than the estimation and time series models are one of the few statistical methods where researches have been stressed on the prediction of future behaviours.

The most important time series models which have been studied in software reliability context are autoregressive processes and moving average processes. Also a more general class called autoregressive moving average time series which contains the above two models has been considered by some authors, see e.g. Davies et al. (1987).

An autoregressive process is a sequential process by which we mean that the value of interest at instance n, t_n, depends on the previous values of the series together with a noise factor. Denote by f the functional relationship between the value t_n and the previous observations, t_{n-i}, i≤k, we have that

$$t_n = f(t_{n-1}, t_{n-2}, ..., t_{n-k}) + \varepsilon_n$$

where ε_n is a random variable denoting the random fluctuation of the observed value.

It is usually assumed that the time t_n is a weighted sum of k past observations t_{n-1}, t_{n-2}, ..., t_{n-k}. Thus, if f is linear which is usually the case, we have that

$$t_n = \sum_{i=1}^{k} \alpha_i t_{n-i} + \varepsilon_n, \ for \ all \ n.$$

A moving average process is a special case of the moving summation process. The value t_n at instance n depends on a sum of weighted random quantities, that is

$$t_n = \sum_{i=1}^{q} \beta_i \varepsilon_{n-i}, \ for \ all \ n.$$

A more general class of time series models is a mixture of an autoregressive process and a moving average process. It is called an autoregressive moving average process. This general class of time series models is useful in many cases and has also been applied in analysing some software failure data, see e.g. Davies et al. (1987).

The applications of time series models have been discussed by various authors, see Section 7.3 for some bibliographic notes. Generally speaking, the results seem to be promising and many existing statistical tools can be applied directly. There are also many textbooks in statistics dealing with time series analysis. The book *"Time Series Analysis - Forecasting and Control"* by Box and Jenkins (1976, Wiley, New York) which is widely referred to is a good reference.

7.1.2. Some random coefficient autoregressive models

Horigome et al. (1985) studied a model based on a first order autoregressive process with a random coefficient θ_i. It also provides us with a Bayesian formulation for the selection of a time series model.

Denote by T_i the time to failure of the software after i changes, i=0,1,...n. Assume that T_i is related to T_{i-1} which is reasonable because the software is subjected to only minor changes when a detected fault is corrected. In order to reflect this fact, the dependence may be written as

$$T_i = \delta_i T_{i-1}^{\theta_i}, \quad i=1,2,\ldots,n;$$

where θ_i is a coefficient and δ_i is an uncertainty factor. The relation is recognized as the power law in reliability and biometry. The model will describe reliability growth or decay depending on whether the value of θ_i is greater or less than unity.

By defining

$$Y_i = lnT_i, \quad i=1,2,\ldots,n,$$

we have that the model can be rewritten as

$$Y_i = \theta_i Y_{i-1} + v_i, \quad i=1,2,\ldots,n;$$

where v_i is the natural logarithm of δ_i, that is

$$v_i = ln\delta_i, \quad i=1,2,\ldots,n.$$

For the sake of convenience, δ_i is assumed to be normally distributed with mean 0 and variance σ^2. By the definition, v_i is lognormal, also with parameters 0 and σ^2.

This is a general formulation of a first-order autoregressive process with random coefficient θ_t. Because of the fact that, during the software testing phase, faults are removed and the reliability increases, it is then reasonable to assume that θ_t is stochastically decreasing in t which implies reliability growth. For large t, θ_t tends to approach unity since no further faults are detected and the reliability of the software is not changed.

Note that different choices of models with respect to θ_i, $i \geq 1$, can be made by using different Kalman filter models. Four models presented in Singpurwalla and Soyer (1985) are the following

(i): $\theta_i \in N(\lambda, \sigma_1{}^2)$ *with σ_1 known and*
$\lambda \in N(\mu, \sigma_2{}^2)$ *with σ_2 known;*

(ii): $\theta_i = \theta_{i-1} + w_i$ *and*
$w_i \in N(0, W_i)$ *with W_i known;*

(iii): $\theta_i = \alpha_1 \theta_{i-1} + \alpha_2 \theta_{i-2} + w_i$, *with α_1 and α_2 known,*
and $w_i \in N(0, W_i)$ with W_i known;

(iv): $\theta_i = \alpha \theta_{i-1} + w_i$ *and*
$\alpha \in Uniform[0,1]$,
$w_i \in N(0, W_i)$ *with W_i known.*

Model (i) is a random coefficient autoregressive time series model originally studied by Horigome et al. (1982) and (ii)-(iv) are ramifications of (i) proposed in Singpurwalla and Soyer (1985). Model (ii) is a special case of a Kalman filter model while model (iv) is referred to as an adaptive Kalman filter model.

Inference based on these models has been studied in Singpurwalla and Soyer (1985). For further results on statistical inference based on these models and applications to real software failure data, interested readers are referred to the original paper and the paper by Soyer (1986).

Although the models suggested by Singpurwalla and Soyer (1985) are quite flexible, there are some drawbacks. The lognormality assumption for the times between failures as well as their autoregressive character seems to be superficial. A modification called the judgement-based model has been proposed in Bergman and Xie (1991).

The judgement-based model for software reliability assumes that failure intensities between failures are constant. Note that this is a plausible assumption if the software has not been changed between two failure events and this is related to the Jelinski-Moranda model.

A natural specific judgement-based model for the failure process is to assume that

$$\tilde{\lambda}_0 \in Gamma(a_0, b_0),$$

$$\tilde{\lambda}_i = \theta_i \tilde{\lambda}_{i-1} \text{ for } i > 0,$$

where $\tilde{\lambda}_i$, $i = 0, 1, \ldots$, is the failure intensity between the i:th and (i+1):th failures.

Different assumptions on the θ_i's can be incorporated. For example, the following models may be considered,

(i): *The θ_i, i≥1, are exchangeable,*

(ii): $\theta_i = \theta_{i-1}\delta_i$, *and*
δ_i, *i≥1, are exchangeable.*

Model (i) above may be treated as a generalized geometric "de-eutrophication" model suggested by Moranda (1975) while the second one is an adaptive model which seems to be quite attractive.

7.1.3. A Fourier series model

It has been observed, see e.g. Crow and Singpurwalla (1984), that software failures usually occur in clusters. The reason for this is that failure times are not independent and the clustering may be caused by change in the concentration of the input data and the variation of the operational environment.

In order to model this clustering process, a Fourier series model is proposed in Crow and Singpurwalla (1984) which has shown that the

Fourier models can be used successfully for analysing clustered failure data, especially those with cyclic behaviour. Cyclic variation is quite common in the application phase of the software. Such a cyclic behaviour may stem from the cyclic variation of input data, periodic maintenance of the hardware system, etc.

Denote by ε_i the disturbance term of the process with mean zero. Let t_i, $i=1,2,...,n$, be the times between failures, the model assumes that there is a cyclic function $g(i)$ such that

$$t_i = g(i) + \varepsilon_i, \quad i=1,2,...,n.$$

This means that the times between failures are deterministic functions of the number of failures caused by random disturbances. More specifically, for odd n, the Fourier series model assumes that $g(i)$ is a linear combination of sine and cosine terms, that is, for all i,

$$g(i) = \alpha_0 + \sum_{j=1}^{q} \left[\alpha(k_j) cos\left(\frac{2\pi}{n}k_j i\right) + \beta(k_j) sin\left(\frac{2\pi}{n}k_j i\right) \right].$$

In the above equation

$$q = \frac{(n-1)}{2}.$$

The estimates of the parameters α_0, $\alpha(k_j)$ and $\beta(k_j)$ may be obtained using the method of least squares. They are given by

$$\widehat{\alpha_0} = \sum_{i=1}^{n} \frac{t_i}{n},$$

$$\widehat{\alpha(k_j)} = \sum_{i=1}^{n} \frac{2t_i}{n} cos\left(\frac{2\pi}{n}k_j i\right), \quad j=1,2,...,q,$$

$$\widehat{\beta(k_j)} = \sum_{i=1}^{n} \frac{2t_i}{n} sin\left(\frac{2\pi}{n}k_j i\right), \quad j=1,2,...,q.$$

The analysis of the failure data and the validation of the model is carried out by studying the so-called spectrogram of the series. By plotting

$$\rho^2(k_j) = \alpha^2(k_j) + \beta^2(k_j)$$

versus the frequency k_j/n for $j=1,2,...,q$, the so-called spectrogram is obtained. The spectrogram of this model provides useful information of a possibly clustered software failure process.

If the spectrogram shows a large value at some k_j, that is if $\rho(k_j)$ is large for some k_j, then k_j/n may be interpreted as a frequency of the cyclic variation of the data. Otherwise, if $\rho(k_j)$ is equally large for all k_j, then no clustering seems to have occurred. Other detailed analysis and applications are presented in Crow and Singpurwalla (1984).

7.2. Regression models

Usually there are several factors affecting software reliability. These factors may be the complexity metrics of the software or the development environment conditions. Regression analysis which utilizes explanatory variables is then an applicable technique for software reliability analysis. In this section we discuss the application of general regression techniques and the Cox proportional hazard models which have been discussed in software reliability context by various authors.

7.2.1. Some general regression models

Regression analysis is another statistical technique which has a great potential in analysing software failure data. It is assumed that there is a relationship between the software reliability and other influential factors during software development.

Let y denote the attribute of interest and assume that x is the explanatory variable which may be a vector consisting of a number of elements x_1, x_2, ... , x_n. If the relation between y and x may be described by a systematic function f(x) subject to a random fluctuation ε, that is

$$y = f(x) + \varepsilon,$$

then the regression of y on x is the equation y=f(x) where it is assumed that ε has zero expectation.

If f(x) is a linear function, the regression is also called a linear regression. Generally we may also consider the case when f(x) is a polynomial. Also, other forms of the regression equation f(x) are possible. The functional form of f(x) depends on the particular circumstance and should be able to describe the dependence between the variable of interest and the explanatory variable x.

Usually, there are a number of parameters in the regression equation to be determined using collected data. The most frequently used method is the method of least squares.

Suppose that a data set is given in form of $\{y_i, x_i; i=1,2,...,n\}$, then the method of least squares is to minimize the squared discrepancies between the observed values y_i and the expected value given by $f(x_i)$, that is

$$S = \sum_{i=1}^{n} [y_i - f(x_i)]^2.$$

In standard literature on statistics, many other statistical properties may be found.

7.2.2. Proportional hazard models

In this section we present some proportional hazard models which may be considered as special cases of the regression models. In particular, we will discuss the application of the Cox proportional hazard model and some of its generalizations which have been used by various authors in analysing software failure data.

The Cox proportional hazard model assumes that the failure intensity is an exponential function of the explanatory variables. That is, the following holds

$$r(t, x) = r_0(t) exp\{\beta_1 x_1 + \beta_2 x_2 + ... + \beta_m x_m\},$$

where x_i's are the explanatory variables and β_i's are the corresponding regression coefficients. In the above, $r_0(t)$ is a baseline failure intensity function that expresses the failure intensity when all explanatory variables are set to zero.

The reliability function is given by

$$R(t, x) = [R_0(t)]^{exp\{\beta_1 x_1 + \beta_2 x_2 + \ldots + \beta_m x_m\}},$$

where $R_0(t)$ is the baseline reliability function given by

$$R_0(t) = exp\left\{-\int_0^t r_0(s)ds\right\}.$$

Historically, the Cox proportional hazard model has been successfully used in analysing biomedical data. Only recently has it been applied in reliability analysis by some researchers. Since software reliability is strongly affected by many factors during the software development, proportional hazard models are helpful tools also in analysing software failure data.

The advantage of using the proportional hazard model is that explanatory variables may be used and information about them can be utilized. Also, it should be pointed out here that different sets of software failure data may be combined by adding a new explanatory variable describing the main difference between the data sets provided that other underlying assumptions are identical.

The explanatory variables x_i's should be chosen so that they are strongly correlated to the failure data. Some examples, useful in software reliability studies, are program size, testing resource allocated, competence of the programmer, programming language etc.

The estimation of the regression parameters can be carried out by using the so-called partial likelihood approach which has the similar asymptotic properties as the usual maximum likelihood approach, but simpler. See e.g. the papers by Ascher (1986) and Mazzuchi et al. (1989) for some further discussions and references.

In practice, the number of explanatory variables may be unlimited although the estimation efforts prevent us from using too many parameters. Also, as pointed out previously, the values of the explanatory variables should be obtained accurately, which is a problem in practice since there is no commonly accepted standard for software data collection. Usually, values of many explanatory variables, even those of great importance, have not been collected. Hence, there is a need to specify a data collection procedure in order to make statistical analysis of software reliability in practical applications.

A direct generalization of the proportional hazard model presented above is to allow the explanatory variables x_i to be a function of time. Usually, this is desirable since they are also subjected to changes and variations. The general formulation is that the relation between the failure intensity and the time varying explanatory variable is given by

$$r(t,x) = r_0(t)\, exp\{\beta_1 x_1(t) + \beta_2 x_2(t) + ... + \beta_m x_m(t)\}.$$

A more general form is the following

$$r(t,x) = r_0(t)\, g(x(t)).$$

In order to estimate the baseline failure intensity function $r_0(t)$, we may use either a parametric approach or a distribution-free approach. An advantage of the proportional hazard technique is that by using a non-parametric approach, the distributional form of the life times may be checked.

Note that in fact, the only assumption made in the proportional hazard model is that the explanatory variables have multiplicative effect on the total hazard function. No other assumptions on the underlying distributions are necessary and this property of PHM makes it useful in software reliability analysis. However, in order to assess the capability of this type of models, further researches have to be conducted.

7.3. Bibliographic notes

It is not until recently that the application of statistical data analysis techniques has been studied. Application of general time series models to software reliability analysis have been studied by Dale and Harris (1982), Soyer (1986) and Davies et al. (1987).

Models presented in Section 7.1.2 and 7.1.3 are discussed in Crow and Singpurwalla (1984), Singpurwalla and Soyer (1985) and Soyer (1986). See also Bergman and Xie (1991) for some further discussions.

General exploratory approach to software reliability analysis has been discussed in Bendell (1986), Walls and Bendell (1986) and McCollin et al. (1989).

Applications of proportional hazard techniques are discussed in Ascher (1986), Wightman and Bendell (1986a), (1986b) and Mazzuchi et al. (1989).

There are some other statistical data analysis techniques worth mentioning here. Dale and Harris (1982) presented some results of application of credibility theory originating from the insurance field. Informatic approaches based on the maximum entropy principle and minimum cross-entropy principle have been studied in De Neumann (1987) and Anderson (1987), Brown (1987) and Ho et al. (1989).

Application of martingale and filtering theory to software reliability analysis has been studied in Koch and Speij (1983) where a framework to obtain software reliability models is discussed. Kenett and Pollak (1986) proposed a semi-parametric model for software reliability growth. A non-parametric approach based on complete monotonicity has been used in Miller and Sofer (1985), (1986).

8

Determination of Optimum Release Time

Usually, it is not enough just to determine the reliability of the software by using a software reliability model. Software products have to be debugged in order to meet the requirement of the reliability which is one of the most important goals of software testing. During the testing phase, one would like to determine when to stop the testing of the software and start to sell the software product. In this chapter, we discuss some existing software release policies and review some important advances in determination of optimum release policies using existing software reliability models. The software release time problem is first formulated as a general optimization problem. Based on some simple software reliability models, we discuss the problem of determination of an optimum release time using different reliability requirements such as the acceptable number of remaining software faults or the acceptable software failure occurrence rate. Usually the problem is to determine whether to release the software or to continue with the testing and it is called a stopping rule problem. Cost models which are important in studying the software life-cycle cost may be incorporated in obtaining other optimum release policies. Further, we will discuss some other issues related to software release problems based on the existing software reliability models. We end this chapter with some bibliographic notes.

8.1. Release problem as an optimization problem

It is important in practice to be able to determine when a software product can be released. Software release problem is one of the most important areas of the application of software reliability models. The goal of software testing is to achieve a reliability requirement before the time to release, but there are other important problems to be considered here.

The longer the software is tested, the more reliable it tends to be. But as for other products, it is important to start the sale of the software products as early as possible. A delay in the release of the software may result in a loss of market share which finally leads to a reduced productivity and decreased economic benefit of the products. It is thus desirable to be able to determine a testing time which is optimum in some sense and the determination of software release time should generally be formulated as an optimization problem.

In order to formulate the optimization problem, different criteria can be identified. First of all, if the requirement is a fault-free software or any other reliability goal to be reached, then the problem is to determine the minimal testing time to reach this reliability requirement, see Figure 8.1. The reliability of the software increases due to the removal of detected software faults. At the beginning, it is less than the required level and the software release time may be determined as the test time needed to reach that level.

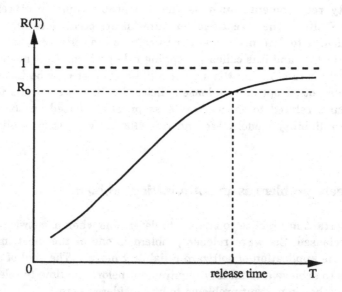

Figure 8.1. The software may be released when its
reliability has reached an acceptable level.

A reliability requirement is often an important specification of the software and the required reliability level has sometimes to be reached before the software can be sold at all. Testing of the software should always be continued until the failure intensity has reached a satisfactory level.

On the other hand, if the total cost of the software has to be considered, then the optimum release time must be determined by using an appropriate cost function which describes the cost development through the whole life-cycle of the software. In that case, the expected total software cost can be minimized using this cost function together with any software reliability model.

Usually, the cost of the testing which includes the cost of the delay in release is an increasing function of time. The cost of the unreliability is, on the other hand, a decreasing function of time because the reliability is an increasing one due to the detecting and removing of software faults. The sum of these two cost functions is thus a U-shaped function for which a minimum exists under some general conditions, see Figure 8.2.

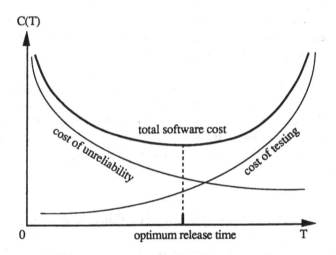

Figure 8.2. The software cost function is a sum of the cost of unreliability and the cost of software testing.

A combination of the above criteria is sometimes possible and in that case we have both a reliability requirement to be reached and a cost function to be minimized. This is sometimes called cost-reliability software release problem and has been studied by various authors.

Usually, parameters, such as those in the reliability models and in the cost functions, are estimated by using earlier collected data. The estimation is often inaccurate and the estimates should be revised when more failure data are available. New estimates of the parameters shall then be used in obtaining a new release policy and hence the procedure should be made as a sequential procedure.

Another problem concerning the software release problem is that the release time may already be set when writing the contract. In that case, the determination of optimum testing time is still interesting because of the following reasons. The actual CPU-time spent in testing may be decreased by increasing the test intensity or test effectiveness, e.g. by using more testing effort such as more testing personnel. This is especially necessary in order to increase the reliability of the software so that the acceptable level of reliability can be reached at the time of release. On the other hand, if an earlier release is possible because the reliability goal has been achieved earlier, then it should be determined from a cost-benefit point of view whether to have more testing or to release earlier.

Concerning the release time issue, there are many other problems involved in practice. However, here we will only consider the case when an optimum release time of the software has to be determined. Other problems such as the optimum software resource allocation problem may easily be solved by using some appropriate modifications of the existing methodologies.

8.2. Optimum release time based on reliability criteria

The main goal of software testing is to obtain a reliable software by detecting and removing software faults. Usually, we have some requirements on the reliability of the software product and this goal has to be reached before the software can be released. In this section, we will study some software release policies which minimize the time needed to reach a reliability requirement.

8.2.1. Stopping rules using the number of remaining faults

Although the number of software faults is not an important measure from a reliability point of view, some investigation of it is necessary. Software release time may easily be determined by requiring that the number of remaining faults has reached a prescribed low level. This general problem has also some statistical interests.

Suppose that we will determine whether to release the software or to continue with the testing and denote by n the number of faults detected up to the present time. If a perfect software, i.e. a software which contains no further faults, is required, a reasonable stopping rule must be to stop testing for the first n such that

$$P(\widehat{N}_0 > n) \le \rho_0,$$

where $\widehat{N}_0$ is the estimated number of initial faults and ρ_0 is a prescribed acceptable risk which is the acceptable probability that the software contains one or more faults.

Caspi and Kouka (1984) presented a sequential stopping rule for software debugging based on some software reliability models. Using the Jelinski-Moranda model the following decision problem may be formulated. Assume that the failure data set $\tilde{t} = \{t_1, t_2, ..., t_n\}$ is given, we should decide among the infinite set of hypotheses $\overline{N} = 0$, $\overline{N} = 1$, $\overline{N} = 2$, ..., which one is true, where $\overline{N}$ is the number of remaining faults. Note that an estimate of $\overline{N}$ is just $\widehat{N}_0 - n$.

It may be noted that this is a more general problem than the classical Wald's sequential probability ratio test problem where the number of hypotheses is assumed to be two. This is hence an interesting statistical decision problem requiring further investigation.

One of the earliest papers dealing with software release time problems is due to Forman and Singpurwalla (1977). Based on the Jelinski-Moranda model the problem of determination of an optimum stopping time is studied. It is found that the optimum time of testing based on the usual maximum likelihood estimate of the number of remaining faults is not suitable because of the instability of the maximum likelihood estimators, see Section 3.2.3 for some discussions.

The relative likelihood function of N_0 is then suggested to be used. The relative likelihood function is defined as

$$L_r(N_0) = \frac{L\left(N_0, \hat{\phi}(N_0)\right)}{L\left(\hat{N}_0, \hat{\phi}\right)},$$

where the nominator is the maximum of the likelihood function given N_0 and the denominator is the unconditional maximum of the likelihood function. Hence $L_r(N_0)$ measures the relative likelihood of the different values of N_0 and it can be used to isolate misleading estimates of N_0.

The relative likelihood function is suggested to be compared with an approximate normal relative likelihood for N_0 which is defined as

$$R(N_0) = exp\left\{-\frac{(\hat{N}_0 - N_0)^2}{2\, Var(\hat{N}_0)}\right\}$$

where $Var(\hat{N}_0)$ is given by

$$Var(\hat{N}_0) = \frac{n}{\left[n\Sigma_{i=1}^n\left(\frac{1}{N_0-i+1)}\right)^2 - \left(\Sigma_{i=1}^n\frac{1}{N_0-i+1}\right)^2\right]}$$

which is the variance given by the classical Cramér-Rao bounds using the standard large sample theory.

The stopping rule by Forman and Singpurwalla (1977) is given as follows

(1) Calculate the maximum likelihood estimate of N_0;

(2) If this estimate of N_0 is close to the number of detected faults n, proceed to step 3, otherwise observe another failure and go back

to step 1;

(3) Calculate the relative likelihood function and compare it with the corresponding normal relative likelihood function. If the plot of the two shows a large disparity, observe another failure and go to step 1. If it shows a good agreement, then testing may be stopped.

In another paper, Forman and Singpurwalla (1979) presented a stopping rule based on statistical theory of hypothesis. Denote by $\overline{N}$ the number of remaining faults after the testing as before. The hypotheses are

$$H_0: \overline{N} = 0, \quad vs. \quad H_1: \overline{N} = r > 0 .$$

Their procedure is to test the software for an additional time t_a and reject H_0 if a failure is encountered. For such a test the type I error which is the probability of rejecting H_0 when it is true is zero since no failure can occur when there is no fault left in the software. The Type II error β which is defined as the probability of rejecting H_0 when it is not true, may also be calculated as

$$\beta = P(T \le t_a \mid \overline{N} = r) = 1 - exp\left\{-\phi r t_a\right\}.$$

Note that the power of the test can be made as large as desired by increasing t_a. Also, the user may specify a value for β and we can, by choosing r=1, determine t_a which is given by

$$t_\alpha = - \frac{ln(1-\beta)}{\phi} .$$

An optimum test between the hypothesis $N_0 = n$ and $N_0 > n$ is to stop testing if there is no further failure detected for an additional time $T(n+1)$. Otherwise, the test is continued and a further time interval $T(n+2)$ is observed.

Before the testing starts, we sometime have to determine a time at which the software may be released. In this case, the amount of testing time needed to reach a reliability requirement has to be determined prior to the testing. This can be done by taking the expected time to remove all of the remaining faults if a fault-free software is required.

In practice, it is not reasonable to test the software until all faults are detected and removed. A possibility is to stop testing when the number of the remaining faults is less than a prescribed number. Another possibility, which is perhaps more reasonable, is to stop the testing when the number of remaining faults is less than a prescribed portion of the number of initial faults. Such a release policy has been studied in Angus et al. (1980).

Assuming that the Jelinski-Moranda model is valid and the parameters have been estimated by using previously collected data. Denote by $T_{(k)}$ the time needed to remove k faults. Then by the assumptions of the model, the expected time of $T_{(k)}$ is given by

$$ET_{(k)} = \sum_{i=1}^{k} \frac{1}{\phi(N_0 - i + 1)}.$$

Hence, testing may be stopped at the time $ET_{(k)}$ given above. This release policy may be generalized to other Markov models, see e.g. Xie (1979).

For NHPP models, because of the existence of mean value functions, it is convenient to determine the time needed to remove a given portion of software faults. Suppose that the parameters of the mean value function have been estimated and a prescribed portion of initial faults are to be detected and removed, then the optimum release time may be determined based entirely on m(t).

For example, assuming that the Goel-Okumoto NHPP model is valid and the parameters are estimated, if the testing is to be stopped when the expected time that 100q percent of faults are removed, then, by using the mean value function of the Goel-Okumoto model, it can be shown that the optimum time to stop testing t_q is

$$t_q = \frac{ln(1-q)}{b}.$$

Note that t_q depends only on the parameter b which characterizes the growth rate of the reliability by debugging. The parameter a in the GO-model, which is the number of faults eventually detected, is not interesting here because we are interested in the percentage of detected faults.

8.2.2. Stopping rules using the failure intensity requirements

As we noted before, the number of software faults which is a practical measure is not a good measure of software reliability and it is interesting mainly from a theoretical point of view. A better choice is the failure intensity function. Hence, to release a software or not at time t should be determined by whether its current failure intensity has reached an acceptable low level.

Denote by $\hat{\lambda}(n+1)$ the estimated occurrence rate of the next failure, here n is the number of detected faults up to the present time. Then the stopping rule is to stop testing when

$$\hat{\lambda}(n+1) \leq \lambda_0,$$

for some prescribed value of λ_0. Note that, if the time to next failure is exponential, the value of λ_0 may be determined through either of the requirements

(i): *The expected time to next failure* $\leq T_0$;

(ii): $P(Time\ to\ next\ failure \leq T_0) \leq \rho_0$.

In the above, T_0 is a prescribed acceptable time to the next failure and ρ_0 is a prescribed acceptable risk.

Okumoto and Goel (1980) presented a simple procedure for the determination of an optimum release time based on the reliability criterion. The underlying software reliability model is the Goel-Okumoto model. Suppose that the parameters are estimated using previous failure data, then the reliability after t_s time of testing is

$$R(t+t_s|t_s) = exp\{-[m(t+t_s)-m(t)]\}.$$

Note that this is generally valid for all NHPP models with mean value function m(t). Using the mean value function of the Goel-Okumoto model, that is by inserting

$$m(t) = a(1 - e^{-bt}),$$

we get that the reliability $R(t+t_s \mid t_s)$ may be expressed as

$$R(t+t_s \mid t_s) = exp\{-m(t)e^{-bt_s}\}.$$

From the above, we can easily determine that the optimum testing time needed to reach a prescribed reliability R, is given by

$$t_s = \frac{1}{b}\{ln[m(t)] - ln[-lnR]\} = \frac{1}{b}\{ln[a(1-e^{-bt})] - ln[-lnR]\}.$$

The above approach may be generalized to other NHPP models as pointed out before. By using other mean value functions, other optimum release policies may be calculated, see e.g. Yamada and Osaki (1986).

Another stopping rule considering the failure intensity requirement has been proposed by Ross (1985b) by using a "quality control" philosophy. Denote by H the acceptable failure intensity after the release and let $\Lambda(t)$ be the current failure intensity of the software. Since $\Lambda(t)$ is unknown, it has to be estimated, for example, by using the estimator proposed in Ross (1985b).

Given an estimate of $\Lambda(t)$, the stopping rule is to stop testing at time t such that

$$\hat{\Lambda}(t) + z_\alpha \sqrt{E\left[\left(\hat{\Lambda}(t) - \Lambda(t)\right)^2\right]} \leq H,$$

where z_α is the α-normal quantile determined by

$$\frac{1}{\sqrt{2\pi}} \int_{2\alpha}^{\infty} exp\{-x^2/2\} dx = \alpha.$$

Other interesting results may be found in the original paper by Ross (1985b). Due to the theoretical complexity, similar approaches have not been widely discussed and this is a topic for further research.

8.3. Optimum policy based on cost criterion

In practice, software release time is associated with the cost of software testing and the gain of an earlier release of the software. Usually, a software manager wants to be able to determine the optimum testing time from a cost-benefit point of view. In this section, we present some cost models and discuss some release policies based on these cost functions. The expected cost of the software in its lifetime is an essential topic. Although the software life-cycle has a finite length, we assume that, for the sake of convenience, this is infinite because for many commercial software the life expectancy is much longer than the testing time. Generally, for finite life-cycle case, only some minor modifications are necessary in order to apply the results directly. Interested readers are referred to a recent paper by Yun and Bai (1990) where modifications of some existing release policies are discussed under a more general assumption that the life-cycle of the software has a random length.

8.3.1. Application of a simple cost model

It seems that Okumoto and Goel (1980) is the first published paper dealing with the release problem considering the cost-benefit of the software. The underlying software reliability model considered in Okumoto and Goel (1980) is the Goel-Okumoto NHPP model. A simple software release model has been presented in that paper and this simple cost function which may be a good approximation of the reality has been further studied together with other software reliability models by various authors.

Denote as usual by m(t) the mean value function of the Goel-Okumoto model, the expected cost of the software product released at time T may be calculated by using the following cost function

$$c(T) = c_1 m(T) + c_2 \left[m(\infty) - m(T) \right] + c_3 T.$$

In the above

c_1 = the expected cost of removing a fault during testing
c_2 = the expected cost of removing a fault during operation
c_3 = the expected cost per unit time of software testing including the cost of testing, the cost due to a delay in releasing the software, etc.

Note that the expected cost of fixing a fault after release is usually higher than the expected cost of fixing a fault during testing. Hence, we assume that $c_2 > c_1$. This is also a general condition for the existence of a positive solution of the optimum release time problem. Otherwise, if the solution is negative, there is no need of having the software tested.

An optimum release policy can generally be found by minimizing the expected total cost function with respect to T. The existence of an optimum release time under very general conditions is obvious, see e.g. Figure 8.2.

The expected cost of removing faults during the testing is $c_1 m(T)$ and this is an increasing function of T because m(T) is increasing. The expected cost of fixing faults during the operational phase is $c_2[m(\infty)-m(T)]$ and this is a deceasing function of T. The expected cost of testing the software for T time units is $c_3 T$. By summing up these cost factors, we get the expected total cost given above.

By differentiating c(T) with respect to T we get that

$$\frac{dc(T)}{dT} = c_1 m'(T) - c_2 m'(T) + c_3$$

and by equating it to zero we obtain

$$m'(T) = \frac{c_3}{c_2 - c_1}.$$

Note also that this is valid for all NHPP models with mean value function m(t). An optimum release time may be determined by solving the above equation.

Using the mean value function of the Goel-Okumoto model we simply get the following equation for the determination of an optimum release time T,

$$abe^{-bT} = \frac{c_3}{c_2 - c_1}.$$

It can be seen that the optimum release time then exists and is unique if

$$ab = \frac{c_3}{c_2 - c_1}$$

and the optimum time T_0 is given by

$$T_o = \frac{1}{b} ln \frac{ab(c_2 - c_1)}{c_3}.$$

Note that if the reversed inequality above holds, then $T_0 < 0$ and since $T_0 \geq 0$, that is an optimum test time is nonnegative, this implies that no testing is necessary. Also, if there is an equality, then $T_0 = 0$ and no testing is needed.

8.3.2. Some general formulations

There are two ways to generalize the results in the above section. Other software reliability models can easily be incorporated. As noted previously, different m(t) can be used together with the simple cost function. Some examples using other types of NHPP models as the underlying failure process model may be found in Yamada and Osaki (1986).

As an example, we may consider the two-type of faults model due to Yamada et al. (1985). Using the simple cost function by Okumoto and Goel (1980) optimum release policy has been studied in Catuneanu et al. (1988). Since the model assumes that there are two types of software faults, two sets of cost functions are used, that is, it is assumed that

$$c(T) = \sum_{i=1}^{2} \{c_{1i} m_i(T) + c_{2i}[m_i(\infty) - m_i(T)] + c_{3i} T\}.$$

In the above, index i denotes that the quantity is specified for type i fault, i=1,2. Using this model, an optimum release time may be obtained by minimizing the above cost function. The optimization may be carried out in a similar manner as before. Similar results on the existence and uniqueness of optimum release time can be obtained.

The original release time policy under the assumption of the two-type of faults model has been previously discussed in Yamada and Osaki (1986), (1987a). The interested readers are also referred to a recent paper by Kapur and Garg (1990b) where the original two-type faults model is modified by allowing imperfect fault-removal.

Another possibility is to generalize the simple cost function by incorporating other cost factors. A generalization of the simple cost function has been proposed by Koch and Kubat (1983). Also, it is possible to combine these two ways. An interesting generalization of the simple cost function has been discussed in Yamada et al. (1984b). It is assumed that there is a scheduled released time of the software. A penalty cost is associated to the total cost function if the software is released after the predetermined delivery time. It is also assumed that the scheduled delivery time is random with a general cumulative distribution function G(t). The expected cost for a delay during $[T_s, T]$ is then given by

$$\int_0^T c_p(T-t) dG(t),$$

hence, the total expected software cost is given by

$$c(T) = c_1 m(T) + c_2[m(\infty) - m(T)] + c_3 T + \int_0^T c_p(T-t) dG(t).$$

Optimum software release time may then be determined by minimizing this cost function. Different special cases have been studied by Yamada et al. (1984b). See also Kapur and Garg (1989) for some further discussions.

Software release policies are often considered as the determination of the time to terminate the software testing. However, it is sometimes possible to stop the testing when a prescribed number of faults are detected. In this case time is not an essential parameter.

Bai and Yun (1988) studied optimum release time based on the optimum number of faults removed before the software testing is terminated. The criterion used is the average gain of the system. Note that the gain of the software may be defined as the negative cost, thus maximizing the gain is equivalent to minimizing the cost.

If the number of initial faults is known or has been estimated using previously collected failure data, then the average gain is given by

$$G(N) = (c_2 - c_1)N - c_3 ET_N,$$

where c_3 is the expected testing cost, c_2 is the average cost of removing a fault during operation and c_1 is the average cost of correcting a fault during testing.

The optimum number of faults removed before releasing the software is then determined by maximizing the above function with respect to N. It can be shown that N is uniquely given by this procedure. Even for the case of unknown N, the procedure is applicable and gives unique optimum value of N under some general assumptions.

Usually, optimum release policies depend only on c_3 and $(c_1 - c_2)$. In Xie (1989) some simplifications using two cost functions are studied using the DFI Markov model. Interested readers are referred to the original paper and the paper by Xie (1991).

8.4. Other optimum release policies

There are many other software release problems in practice. The importance of studying optimum release policy has now been recognized since the determination of when to stop testing and release the software involves many different problems. There are several new directions where further researches are needed and in this section we briefly review some recent results.

8.4.1. Minimizing the expected cost given a reliability goal

Usually optimum release policies have to be determined based on both cost and reliability requirements simultaneously. This is a topic which has interested various authors, see e.g. Goel and Okumoto (1981), Yamada and Osaki (1985a) and Kapur and Garg (1989). By combining the results in the above sections, it is easy to calculate an optimum release time by minimizing the total expected cost under the restriction of a reliability requirement. It is also possible to determine optimum release time by maximizing the reliability given the total available testing expenditure.

A common problem in practice is that a prescribed reliability goal has been set and this reliability requirement has to be reached. An optimum release policy has then to be determined by minimizing the expected total cost subjected to this reliability goal. The release time T is in this case determined by solving the following optimization problem.

$$Min\ c(T),\ T{\geq}0,$$

$$subject\ to\ R(x|T){\geq}R_0.$$

Assume that the expected cost $c(T)$ is a convex function and $R(x|T)$ is an increasing function of T which is reasonable because as T increases, more faults are removed and the reliability will increase. Denote by T_0 the time which minimizes the expected cost $c(T)$ and then by computing the minimum time to reach the reliability requirement R_0, we get another time and denote it by T_1. The optimum release time is then

$$T = max\ \{0, T_0, T_1\}$$

Based on other general NHPP models with mean value function m(t), the solution of other cost-reliability optimum software release problems can easily be found. It is obvious that the results of Section 8.2 and 8.3 can be combined in order to obtain an optimum release time which minimizes the expected cost under the assumption that the reliability requirement is satisfied. Such release policies have been widely studied by various authors. See Yamada and Osaki (1987a), Kapur and Garg (1990a) for some recent publications.

It should be noted here that most results on cost-reliability software release problems in existing literature concern with the existence and uniqueness of the optimum release time. They are quite obvious in many cases under the general assumption that the cost of correcting a fault during operation is higher than the corresponding cost during testing. The most difficult problem in practice is the estimation of various unknown parameters, both those in the software reliability models and those in the cost functions. Generally, sequential procedures have to be adopted because the estimates which are inaccurate in many cases, have to be revised, using newly collected data.

8.4.2. Release policy of software with modular structure

Because a software usually consists of a number of modules, software release times should be based on the modular structure of the software. Except some discussions by Littlewood (1979b) and Kubat and Koch (1983), software release problems using modular structure of software have not been widely studied.

An interesting model using a statistical approach for the determination of optimum release time of software with modular structure is proposed in Masuda et al. (1989). The decision is given, under some general assumptions, for the determination of whether the software will be released or further testing for another period of time is necessary.

Suppose that the software has been tested for T time units. An objective function, v(t), which describes the profit by further testing of length t, is used. The objective function is defined as

$$v(t) = v_1(T+t) - v_2(t) - v_3(T+t),$$

where $v_1(\cdot)$ is the expected value of the software at time t, $v_2(\cdot)$ is the average cost due to undetected faults and $v_3(\cdot)$ is the cumulative running cost of testing. Usually, $v_i(\cdot)$, i=1,2,3, contain parameters which are unknown and have to be estimated.

Note that only v_2 depends on the number of remaining faults in the software. The modular software model assumes that each module of the software contains a number of faults which may be very different. It is also assumed that the lifetimes of software faults in one module are independent, identically distributed. For example, for faults with Weibull lifetimes the number of faults in each module may be estimated using collect failure data, see Masuda et al. (1989) for some procedures to do this. Note that the exponential lifetime distribution which corresponds to the Jelinski-Moranda model can be seen as a special case of the Weibull case.

Suppose that the software is composed of k modules and denote by c_i the cost of removing a fault in module i. Also, denote by α_T the portion of time in which the software is used and β_i denotes the portion of the time module i which is executed given that the software is used. The function v_2 used by Masuda et al. (1989) is given by

$$v_2(t) = \sum_{i=1}^{K} \frac{c_i(N_i - r_i)}{1 - F_i(\alpha_T \beta_i T)},$$

where N_i is the number of original faults in module i and r_i is the number of corrected faults. Note that N_i needs to be estimated and a procedure is given in Masuda et al. (1989).

If now all $v_i(t)$, i=1,2,3, are known, then by using the objective function v(t), the value of v at time Δ, $v(\Delta)$, can be calculated and compared to v(0) which is the expected software cost without testing. If $v(0) \geq v(\Delta)$, testing is stopped at once and the software may be released. Otherwise, the software is tested for another time Δ and the whole procedure is repeated.

8.4.3. Release time of versions of software packages

A common situation in practice is that the same software is released several times in different versions. A later version is usually an improved one of the previous software packages. Releasing new versions of the same software is a process that may continue throughout the whole software life-cycle. It is therefore useful to have models to describe such a situation and to provide methodologies for the determination of optimum release policies of software packages. However, such models have not received much attention in literature and it is a topic for further research.

Recently Levin and Yadid (1990) proposed a model for the determination of an optimum release time of new versions of software by using the Goel-Okumoto model for the software failure process. The optimization is carried out by minimizing the expected total software development cost. Four different cost factors associated with the release time problem which are identified are the following.

Firstly, there is always a fixed cost associated with the release of a new version. Such a cost may depend on the number of customers and it includes the cost of documentation, distribution, installation, customer training, etc. Secondly, we have cost factor that determines the expected cost of correcting a fault which is assumed to be proportional to the number of detected faults. For the Goel-Okumoto model with parameter a and b, the expected number of faults detected during time [0,t) is given by $a(1-e^{-bt})$ as before and the sum of these two cost factors are

$$K + c_1 a(1-e^{-bt})$$

where K is the fix cost associated with a new release and c_1 is the average cost of correcting a fault.

According to Levin and Yadid (1990) the cost of improving the software during time (0,t] is given by

$$c_2 v\left(e^{-wt} - 1 + wt\right)w$$

where c_2 is defined as the average cost of responding to a request for improvement and v and w are other model parameters reflecting the dynamic of the requirement of changing. This cost model of the improvement is adopted from economic replacement policies.

Finally, another cost factor which is called the cost of software obsolescence represents the loss of market share since the longer it takes to release a new version, the more customers turn to other competitors. The software obsolescence is given by

$$\frac{c_3 x\left(e^{-yt} - 1 + yt\right)}{y}$$

where c_3 is the opportunity loss of a customer according to the model by Levin and Yadid (1990).

The optimum time to release a new version is then determined by minimizing the total expected cost per unit time which is given by

$$c(t) = \frac{K + c_1 a\left(1 - e^{-bt}\right) + c_2 v\left(e^{-wt} - 1 + wt\right)w + \frac{c_3 x\left(e^{-yt} - 1 + yt\right)}{y}}{t}.$$

The optimum release policy can easily be determined numerically. However, the essential part in this analysis is to obtain values of the parameters used in the model.

The results by Levin and Yadid (1990) are obtained by using conventional software reliability models. In studying the release time of new versions, there are many other important issues. Usually, changes of the software may be known and most of them are due to the requirement changes. All of these factors should be incorporated into sequential release policies. Also models such as the fault-spreading model similar to that discussed in Wohlin and Körner (1990) can be used and this may be a topic for further research.

8.4.4. A sequential Bayes decision model

Generally, software release time problem can be treated as a decision problem. Application of Bayesian decision policies to software reliability analysis is another topic worth further research. An optimum stopping rule has been studied in Dalal and Mallow (1988) based on the trade-off between the cost of continued testing and the expected losses due to the remaining faults. It is assumed that testing costs are of arbitrary form f(t) and the costs of removing faults are known constants both during testing and after the release.

The underlying software reliability model is similar to that of Jewell (1985) and it assumes that the number of initial faults N_0 is an unknown random variable. It is further assumed that N_0 has a Poisson distribution with mean λ which is Gamma distributed. The time of detecting a particular fault is random with a known distribution G of arbitrary form.

Denote by N(t) the number of faults detected during [0,t), the general loss function is given by

$$l(t, N_0, N(t)) = f(t) + c_1 N(t) + c_2[N_0 - N(t)]$$

where c_1 is the average cost of correcting a fault during the testing and c_2 is the average cost of finding a fault during the operation.

Generally, optimum stopping rule has to be determined by iteratively solving a functional differential equation which may be a very difficult task. However, some asymptotic results may be obtained. By using the general loss function and the above assumptions, conditions on the functions f and G that ensure that the optimum stopping rule has a simple form may be found by a dynamic programming argument. The main condition is that

$$f(G^{-1}(1-e^{-y})) \text{ is a convex function of } y.$$

Assume that N_0 is Poisson with known mean λ, the optimum strategy is a fixed time stopping rule. The optimum time to stop testing is given by the nonnegative solution of the following equation

$$f'(t) = (c_2 - c_1)\lambda G'(t)$$

and if the solution is negative, the optimum stopping rule is to stop immediately without further testing.

Now assume that N_0 and λ are variables and large with high probability, then the optimum decision rule has a simple asymptotic form. It is to stop whence the number of observed faults k satisfies the following condition

$$k \le \frac{f'(t)G(t)}{(c_2 - c_1)G'(t)},$$

where $G'(t)$ is the density function of G.

As a special case we may assume that G is exponential with mean μ and $f(t)$ is a linear function of t, that is $f(t) = Bt$ for some constant B. Then the stopping rule is to stop as soon as the following condition is satisfied

$$k \leq \frac{B\left(e^{-\mu} - 1\right)}{\mu(c_2 - c_1)}.$$

It is also indicated in Dalal and Mallows (1988) that the above results do not seriously depend on the Poisson or Gamma assumption for N_0 as long as the process does not terminate quickly. Examples and some further results may be found in the original paper.

8.5. Bibliographic notes

Earlier papers dealing with optimum release time problem are Forman and Singpurwalla (1977), (1979), Okumoto and Goel (1980), Goel and Okumoto (1981), Kaspi and Kouka (1984) and Yamada and Osaki (1985a).

Statistical problems in making decision of software release policies have been discussed in Forman and Singpurwalla (1977), (1979), Caspi and Kouka (1984), Ross (1985b) and Dalal and Mallows (1988).

Optimum release policies based on cost and reliability constraints have been studied by various authors. See the papers by Okumoto and Goel (1980), Goel and Okumoto (1981), Yamada and Osaki (1985a), (1986), (1987a), Kapur and Garg (1989), (1990a) and Xie (1991).

Some other papers discussing optimum software release problems are:

Bai and Yun (1985), Brown et al. (1989), Catuneanu et al. (1988), Chi and Kuo (1990), Kapur and Garg (1990b), (1991a), Koch and Kubat (1983), Levin and Yadid (1990), Masuda et al. (1989), Musa and Ackerman (1989), Ohtera and Yamada (1990), Ohtera et al. (1990a), Shanthikumar and Tufekci (1983), Xie (1989) and Yamada et al. (1984b).

9

Recent Advances in Software Reliability

In this chapter we briefly review some recent advances of software reliability and some related topics which in general terms are included in software engineering and software quality control. However, this cannot be completely done since the problems concern many different areas. The essential topics we will discuss here are the concepts, models and methods for software reliability improvement. Some recent references will also be provided for interested readers for further reading.

9.1. Software engineering techniques

Software engineering is perhaps the fastest developing scientific research area during the last decade. New software reliability models should also be developed by considering the new methodologies and technologies of software engineering, such as different testing strategies and different techniques for fault-avoidance, fault-tolerance and fault-removal.

To increase the reliability, it is important at first hand to avoid making human mistakes by *fault-avoidance*, e.g. by improved development strategy. Well-known methods, such as formal design methods, structured programming and quality assurance techniques can usually be implemented. In order to improve the software development process, a lot of factors have to be considered. Different strategies can also be applied and any improvement design techniques may yield more reliable products.

In practice, due to human unreliability, some mistakes are always made, and by system testing and debugging, we may detect and correct some of these software faults usually caused by human errors. Such an action is often called *fault-removal* and it has the effect to improve the reliability so that a required level of it can be reached. Program proving which is desirable, especially for safety-critical systems, is not generally possible and program testing has proved to be the only alternative to detect the software faults. There are, however, many different testing strategies for the fault-removal purpose. Methods such as module testing, functional testing etc. have been proven to be helpful techniques to detect those software faults still remaining in the software. It is important to incorporate different testing strategies in practice.

Finally, *fault-tolerant* software which will provide correct functional operation in the presence of one or more software faults, should be incorporated into safety-critical systems and researches have been devoted to this field during recent years. The multiversion programming approach and recovery block which are widely applied techniques to mask out the occurrence of software faults have recently interested many authors. From a reliability point of view, software systems are unlike hardware systems for which redundancy can usually be used in order to obtain a more reliable configuration. By using different versions developed by different software teams and by running these versions simultaneously, some redundancy may be achieved. However, unlike hardware systems, software systems usually involve stronger positive dependence which reduces the effectiveness of redundancy.

Software reliability engineering which is a part of software engineering has to be developed considering different software engineering techniques and studies of new engineering methods have been more and more important. It is thus desirable for a software reliability engineer to understand and incorporate the new philosophy of software engineering discipline. Interested readers are referred to the books at the end of this chapter.

9.2. Software quality and reliability engineering

Reliability is traditionally included in a larger area, quality technology. Although reliability is the most important quantitative measure of product quality, since anything has to function properly before talking about other quality measures, weight, portability, readability, etc., these measures have usually to be considered from a cost benefit point of view.

As well as for hardware products, software quality is important for software products. Modern quality engineering is the area of studying product quality with emphases on the quality improvement. For any product, nowadays, quality problems will fail to make the customers satisfied and an increased product quality will increase the productivity and cost-effectiveness by increased customer satisfaction.

There are many techniques proposed and studied for quality improvement in standard literature of quality engineering. Some interesting books on software quality which is a very recent research area may be found at the end of this chapter.

Reliability as a part of quality engineering, has been studied for a long time for hardware systems. However, in software reliability engineering, although many models and methods are proposed, there are several other methods worth further research. Below we briefly discuss some interesting topics related to system safety analysis.

Fault-tree analysis which may be an aid in the analysis of different events that will lead to a system failure has been widely studied and applied in hardware reliability analysis. Applications to software reliability analysis are, however, few. There is a great research potential in this field and especially for safety-critical software systems, such an analysis seems to be necessary. Some attempts can be found in some recent papers by Leveson (1986) and Stålhane (1989).

Software *failure mode, effect (and criticality) analysis (FMEA)* which is another systematic method for safety analysis can be used to identify failure causes and their consequences. Improvement may be based on the criticality analysis which is helpful to measure the importance of different failure causes. A discussion may be found in a relatively early paper by Reifer (1979).

There are other structure reliability models and results which can be very helpful in studying structured software systems based on the modular structure of software. However, for redundant software systems the dependence should be studied further.

Statistical quality control has been successfully applied to hardware products and due to many differences between software and hardware production, this cannot be directly used in software development. However, statistical analysis of failure data seems to be the same, both for software and hardware. During software testing, faults are removed and reliability increases. This book has been devoted to such models.

However, simple methods and analysis techniques are desirable in practical applications. Graphical analysis techniques such as quality control charts, probability plot, total time on test plot, Duane plot, etc. which have been used in hardware quality and reliability engineering may as well be used for software development. Also similar techniques may be developed for software reliability purpose.

9.3. Books for further reading

Anderson, T. and Lee, P.A. (1988). *Fault Tolerance, Principles and Practice*. Springer-Verlag, Berlin.

Bishop, P.G. (1991). *Dependability of Critical Computer Systems*. Vol.3. Elsevier, London.

Kitchenham, B.A. and Littlewood, B. (1987). *Measurement for Software Control and Assurance*. Elsevier, London.

Musa, J.D. et al. (1987). *Software Reliability: Measurement, Prediction, Application*. McGraw-Hill, New York.

Rook, P. (1990). *Software Reliability Handbook*. Elsevier, London.

Shooman, M.L. (1983). *Software Engineering: Design, Reliability, Management*. McGraw-Hill, New York.

Smith, D.J. and Wood, K.B. (1989). *Engineering Quality Software*. Elsevier, London.

References

Abdel-Ghaly, A.A. et al. (1986). Evaluation of competing software reliability predictions. *IEEE Trans. Software Eng.*, SE-12, 950-967.

Adrion, W.R. et al. (1982). Validation, verification, and testing of computer software. *ACM Computing Surveys*, 14, 159-192.

Akiyama, F. (1971). An example of software system debugging. *Proc. IFIP Congress, Vol.1*, North-Holland, Amsterdam, pp.353-359.

Amster, S.J. and Shooman, M.L. (1975). Software reliability: an overview. In *Reliability and Fault Tree Analysis*, Eds. R.E. Barlow, J.B. Fussell and N.D. Singpurwalla, SIAM, Philadelphia, pp.655-685.

Anderson, B.G. (1987). The role for entropy and information in software reliability. In *Software Reliability: Achievement and Assessment*, Ed. B. Littlewood, Blackwell, Oxford, pp.172-191.

Angus, J.E. et al. (1980). Software reliability model validation. *Proc. Ann. Reliability and Maintainability Symp.*, pp.191-198.

Arlat, J. et al. (1990a). Dependability modelling and evaluation of software fault-tolerant systems. *IEEE Trans. Computers*, C-39, 504-513.

Arlat, J. et al. (1990b). Fault injection for dependability validation: a methodology and some applications. *IEEE Trans. Software Eng.*, SE-16, 166-182.

Ascher, H. (1986). The use of regression techniques for matching reliability models to the real world. In *Software System Design Methods*, Ed. J.K. Skwirzynski, NATO ASI Series, Vol.F22, Springer-Verlag, Berlin, pp.366-378.

Ashrafi, N. et al. (1990). Proposed structure for decomposition software reliability prediction model. *Information and Software Techn.*, 32, 93-98.

Avizienis, A. (1985). The N-version approach to fault-tolerant software. *IEEE Trans. Software Eng.*, SE-11, 1491-1501.

Bai, D.S. and Yun, W.Y. (1988). Optimum number of errors corrected before releasing a software system. *IEEE Trans. Reliability*, R-37, 41-45.

Bailey, C.T. and Dingee, W.L. (1981). A software study using Halstead metrics. *ACM/Sigmetrics*, 10, 189-197.

Balakrishnan, M. and Raghavendra, C.S. (1990). On reliability modeling of closed fault-tolerant computer systems. *IEEE Trans. Computers*, C-39, 571-575.

Barlow, R.E. and Singpurwalla, N.D. (1985). Assessing the reliability of computer software and computer networks: an opportunity for partnership with computer scientists. *The American Statistician*, 39, 88-94.

Barton, J.H. et al. (1990). Fault injection experiments using FIAT. *IEEE Trans. Computers*, C-39, 575-582.

Bastani, F.B. and Ramamoorthy, C.V. (1986). Input-domain-based models for estimating the correctness of process control programs. In *Reliability Theory*, Eds. A. Serra and R.E. Barlow, North-Holland, Amsterdam, pp.321-378.

Bastani, F.B. and Ramamoorthy, C.V. (1989). Software reliability. In *Handbook of Statistics*, Vol.7, Eds. P.R. Krishnaiah and C.R. Rao, Elsevier, London, pp.7-25.

Becker, G. and Camarinopoulos, L. (1990). A Bayesian estimation method for the failure rate of a possibly correct program. *IEEE Trans. Software Eng.*, SE-16, 1307-1310.

Belli, F. (1990). Fault-tolerant program and their reliability. *IEEE Trans. Reliability*, R-39, 184-192.

Belli, F. and Jedrzejowicz, P. (1989). Towards reliability optimization of fault-tolerant software. *J. Information Processing and Cybernetics*, 24, 431-442.

Bendell, T. (1986). The use of exploratory data analysis techniques for software reliability assessment and prediction. In *Software System Design Methods*, Ed. J.K. Skwirzynski, NATO ASI Series, Vol.F22, Springer-Verlag, pp.337-351.

Bendell, T. and Mellor, P. (1986). *Software Reliability: State of the Art Report*. Pergamon Infotech Ltd., London.

Bergman, B. and Xie, M. (1991). On software reliability modelling. *J. Statistical Planning and Inference*, to appear.

Bishop, P.G. and Pullen, F.D. (1988). Probabilistic modelling of software failure characteristics. In *SAFECOM'88: Safety Related Computers in an Expanding Market*, Ed. W.D. Ehrenberger, pp.87-93.

Bishop, P.G. et al. (1987). STEM - a project on software test and evaluation methods. In *Achieving Safety and Reliability with Computer Systems*, Ed. B.K. Daniels, Elsevier, London, pp.100-117.

Bittanti, S. et al. (1988a). An introduction to software reliability modelling. In *Software Reliability Modelling and Identification*, Ed. S. Bittanti, Springer-Verlag, Berlin, pp.43-67.

Bittanti, S. et al. (1988b). A flexible modelling approach for software reliability growth. In *Software Reliability Modelling and Identification*, Ed. S. Bittanti, Springer-Verlag, Berlin, pp.101-140.

Bittanti, S. et al. (1988c). Parameter identification for software reliability growth models. *Proc. 8th IFAC Symp. on Identification and System Parameter Estimation*, Aug.27-31, Beijing, China.

Bowen, J.B. (1987). Application of a multi-model approach to estimating residual software faults and time between failures. *Quality and Reliability Eng. International*, 3, 41-51.

Brocklehurst, S. et al. (1988). A general adaptive approach to software reliability prediction. *UK IT 88 Conference Publication*, Swansea, U.K., July 4-7, pp.49-52.

Brocklehurst, S. et al. (1990). Recalibrating software reliability models. *IEEE Trans. Software Eng.*, SE-16, 458-470.

Brown, D.B. et al. (1989). A cost model for determining the optimal number of software test cases. *IEEE Trans. Software Eng.*, SE-15, 218-221.

Brown, D.E. (1987). A method for obtaining software reliability measures during development. *IEEE Trans. Reliability*, R-36, 573-580.

Brown, J.R. and Lipow, M. (1975). Testing for software reliability. *Proc. Int. Conf. Reliable Software*, pp.518-527.

Bukowski, J.V. (1987). Evaluating software test results: a new approach. *Proc. Ann. Reliability and Maintainability Symp.*, pp.369-373.

Bunday, B.D. and Al-Ayoubi, I.D. (1990). Likelihood and Bayesian estimation methods for Poisson process models in software reliability. *Int. J. Quality and Reliability Management*, 7, 9-18.

Cai, K.Y. et al. (1991). A critical review on software reliability modeling. *Reliability Eng. and System Safety*, 32, 357-371.

Caruso, J.M. (1991). Integrating prior knowledge with a software reliability growth model. *Proc. 13th Int. Conf. on Software Eng.*, pp.238-245.

Caspi, P.A. and Kouka, E.F. (1984). Stopping rules for a debugging process based on different software reliability models. *Proc. Int. Conf. on Fault-Tolerant Computing*, pp.114-119.

Castillo, X. and Sieworek, D.P. (1982). A workload dependent software reliability prediction model. *Proc. Fault Tolerant Computing Symp.*, pp.279-286.

Catuneanu, V.M. and Mihalache, A.N. (1985). Improving the accuracy of the Littlewood-Verrall model. *IEEE Trans. Reliability*, R-34, 418-421.

Catuneanu, V.M. et al. (1988). Optimal software release policies using SLUMT. *Microelectronics and Reliability*, 28, 547-549.

Catuneanu, V.M. et al. (1991). Optimal software release time with learning rate and testing effort. *IEEE Trans. Reliability*, to appear.

Cavano, J.P. (1984). Software reliability measurement: prediction, estimation, and assessment. *J. Systems and Software*, 4, 269-275.

Chan, P.Y. (1986a). Adaptive models. In *Software Reliability: State of the Art Report*, Eds. A. Bendell and P. Mellor, Pengamon Infotech Ltd., pp.3-18.

Chan, P.Y. (1986b). Stochastic treatment of the failure rate in software reliability growth models. In *Software Reliability: State of the Art Report*, Eds. A. Bendell and P. Mellor, Pengamon Infotech Ltd., pp.19-29.

Chenoweth, H.B. (1991). Reliability prediction, in the conceptual phase of a processor system with its embedded software. *Proc. Ann. Reliability and Maintainability Symp.*, pp.416-422.

Cheung, R.C. (1980). A user oriented software reliability model. *IEEE Trans. Software Eng.*, SE-6, 118-125.

Chi, D.H. and Kuo, W. (1990). Optimal design for software reliability and development cost. *IEEE J. Selected Areas in Commun.*, SAC-8, 276-282.

Chillarege, R. et al. (1991). Defect type and its impact on the growth curve. *Proc. 13th Int. Conf. on Software Eng.*, pp.246-255.

Christodoulakis, D. and Panziou, G. (1990). Modelling software reliability prediction with optimal estimation techniques. *Information and Software Techn.*, 32, 88-92.

O'Connor, P.D.T. (1988). Software Reliability. In *Proc. Arab School on Science and Technology*, Ed. P.D.T. O'Connor, Springer-Verlag, Berlin, pp.175-186.

Corcoran, W.J. et al. (1964). Estimating reliability after corrective action. *Management Science*, 10, 786-795.

Coté, V. et al. (1988). Software metrics: an overview of recent results. *J. Systems and Software*, 8, 121-131.

Coutinho, J.S. (1973). Software reliability growth. *Proc. IEEE Symp. Computer Software Reliability*, pp.58-64.

Cover, D.K. (1988). Issues affecting the reliability of software-cost estimates. *Proc. Ann. Reliability and Maintainability Symp.*, pp.195-201.

Crow, L.H. (1986). Failure patterns and reliability growth potential for software systems. In *Software System Design Methods*, Ed. J.K. Skwirzynski, NATO ASI Series, Vol.F22, Springer-Verlag, Berlin, pp.354-363.

Crow, L.H. and Singpurwalla, N.D. (1984). An empirically developed Fourier series model for describing software failures. *IEEE Trans. Reliability*, R-33, 176-183.

Csenki, A. (1990). Bayes predictive analysis of a fundamental software reliability model. *IEEE Trans. Reliability*, R-39, 177-183.

Currit, P.A. et al. (1986). Certifying the reliability of software. *IEEE Trans. Software Eng.*, SE-12, 3-12.

Dalal, S.R. and Mallows, C.L. (1988). When should one stop testing software. *J. American Statistical Association*, 83, 872-879.

Dalal, S.R. and Mallows, C.L. (1990). Some graphical aids for deciding when to stop testing software. *IEEE Trans. Selected Areas in Commun.*, SAC-9, 168-175.

Dale, C.J. (1986). Software reliability models. In *Software Reliability: State of the Art Report*, Eds. A. Bendell and P. Mellor, Pengamon Infotech Ltd., pp.31-44.

Dale, C.J. (1987). Data requirements for software reliability prediction. In *Software Reliability: Achievement and Assessment*, Ed. B. Littlewood, Blackwell, Oxford, pp.144-153.

Dale, C.J. and Forster, S. (1987). The development of techniques for safety and reliability assessment: past, present and future. In *Achieving Safety and Reliability with Computer Systems*, Ed. B.K. Daniels, Elsevier, pp.141-130.

Dale, C.J. and Harris, L.N. (1982). Approaches to software reliability prediction. *Proc. Ann. Reliability and Maintainability Symp.*, pp.167-175.

Davies, N. et al. (1987). The Musa data revisited: alternative methods and structure in software reliability modelling and analysis. In *Achieving Safety and Reliability with Computer Systems*, Ed. B.K. Daniels, Elsevier, pp.118-130.

Davis, J.S. and LeBlanc, R.J. (1988). A study of the applicability of complexity measures. *IEEE Trans. Software Eng.*, SE-14, 1366-1372.

Dickson, J.C. et al. (1972). Quantitative analysis of software reliability. *Proc. Ann. Reliability and Maintainability Symp.*, pp.148-157.

Downs, T. (1985). An approach to the modeling of software testing with some applications. *IEEE Trans. Software Eng.*, SE-11, 375-386.

Drake, H.D. and Wolting, D.E. (1987). Reliability theory applied to software testing. *Hewlett-Packard Journal*, 4, 35-39.

Dudley, S. (1988). Software reliability. In *Handbook of Reliability Engineering Management*, Eds. W.G. Ireson and C.F. Coombs, Jr., McGraw-Hill, New York, pp.16.1-16.20.

Duran, J.W. and Wiorkowski, J.J. (1981). Capture-recapture sampling for estimating software error content. *IEEE Trans. Software Eng.*, SE-7, 147-148.

Eckhardt, D.E. and Lee, L.D. (1985). A theoretical basis for the analysis of multiversion software subject coincident error. *IEEE Trans. Software Eng.*, SE-11, 1511-1517.

Ehrlich, W.K. and Emerson, T.J. (1987). Modeling software failures and reliability growth during system testing. *Proc. 9th Int. Conf. on Software Eng.*, pp.72-82.

Ehrlich, W.K. et al. (1990a). Applying reliability measurement: a case study. *IEEE Software*, 3, 56-64.

Ehrlich, W.K. et al. (1990b). Application of software reliability modeling to product quality and test process. *Proc. 12th Int. Conf. on Software Eng.*, pp.108-116.

Elliott, R.W. et al. (1978). Measuring computer software reliability. *Computer and Industrial Eng.*, 2, 141-151.

Elspas, B. et al. (1971). Software reliability. *Computer*, 4, 21-27.

Farr, W.H. and Smith, O.D. (1988). A tool for statistical modeling and estimation of reliability functions for software: SMERFS. *J. Systems and Software*, 8, 47-55.

Ferens, D.V. (1986). Computer software reliability prediction. *Proc. IEEE National Aerospace and Electronics Conf.*, Dayton, pp.713-717.

Fiorentino, E. and Soistman, E.C. (1985). Combined hardware software reliability predictions. *Proc. Ann. Reliability and Maintainability Symp.*, pp.169-176.

Forman, E.H. and Singpurwalla, N.D. (1977). An empirical stopping rule for debugging and testing computer software. *J. American Statistical Association*, 72, 750-757.

Forman, E.H. and Singpurwalla, N.D. (1979), Optimal time intervals for testing hypotheses on computer software errors. *IEEE Trans. Reliability*, R-28, 250-253.

Friedman, M. (1987). Modeling the penalty costs of software failure. *Proc. Ann. Reliability and Maintainability Symp.*, pp.359-363.

Gaffney, J.E. Jr. (1984). Estimating the number of faults in code. *IEEE Trans. Software Eng.*, SE-10, 459-464.

Gaudoin, O. and Soler, J.L. (1991). Statistical analysis of a software reliability model. *IEEE Trans. Reliability*, to appear.

Geist, R.M. and Trivedi, K.S. (1983). Ultra-high reliability prediction for fault-tolerant computer systems. *IEEE Trans. Computers*, C-32, 1118-1127.

Gelperin, D. and Hetzel, B. (1988). The growth of software testing. *Communications of the ACM*, 31, 687-695.

Gentzler, G.L. Jr. and Andrews, N.M. (1990). Data stability in an application of a software reliability model. *IEEE J. Selected Areas in Commun.*, SAC-8, 273-280.

Gerig, T.M. and Cook, J.R. (1986). Modeling the reliability of fault-tolerant software systems. *COMPSTAT'86*, Physica-Verlag, Heidelberg.

Ghezzi, C. et al. (1988). On the role of software reliability in software engineering. In *Software Reliability Modelling and Identification*, Ed. S. Bittanti, Springer-Verlag, Berlin, pp.1-42.

Giammo, T. (1986). Relaxation of the common failure rate assumption in modelling software reliability. In *Software Reliability: State of the Art Report*, Eds. A. Bendell and P. Mellor, Pengamon Infotech Ltd., pp.54-79.

Gilb, T. (1977). The measurement of software reliability and maintainability: some unconventional approaches to reliable software. *Computers and People*, September, 16-19.

Goel, A.L. (1980a). Software error detection model with applications. *J. Systems and Software*, 1, 243-249.

Goel, A.L. (1980b). A summary of the discussion on "an analysis of competing software reliability models". *IEEE Trans. Software Eng.*, SE-6, 501-502.

Goel, A.L. (1985). Software reliability models: assumptions, limitations, and applicability. *IEEE Trans. Software Eng.*, SE-11, 1411-1423.

Goel, A.L. and Okumoto, K. (1979). Time-dependent error-detection rate model for software reliability and other performance measures. *IEEE Trans. Reliability*, R-28, 206-211.

Goel, A.L. and Okumoto, K. (1981). When to stop testing and start using software? *ACM/Sigmetrics*, 10, 131-135.

Goel, A.L. and Soenjoto, J. (1981). Models for hardware-software system operational performance evaluation. *IEEE Trans. Reliability*, R-30, 232-239.

Goel, A.L. et al. (1987). An empirical study of FORTRAN and ADA program reliability. *COMPSAC '87*, pp.340-346.

Goseva-Popstojanova, K.D. and Grnarov, A.L. (199). A new Markov model of N version programming systems. *Proc. Int. Symp. on Software Reliability Eng.*, pp.210-217.

Govil, K.K. (1984). Incorporation of execution time concept in several software reliability models. *Reliability Eng.*, 7, 235-249.

Goyal, A. and Lavenberg, S.S. (1987). Modeling and analysis of computer system availability. *IBM J. Research and Development*, 31, 651-664.

Gray, C.T. (1986). A framework for modelling software reliability. In *Software Reliability: State of the Art Report*, Eds. A. Bendell and P. Mellor, Pengamon Infotech Ltd., pp.81-94.

Halstead, M.H. (1977). *Elements of Software Science*. Elsevier, New York.

Hamer, P. (1986). Types of metric. In *Software Reliability: State of the Art Report*, Eds. A. Bendell and P. Mellor, Pengamon Infotech Ltd., pp.95-104.

Hamlet, R.G. (1987). Probable correctness theory. *Information Processing Letters*, 25, 17-25.

Hansen, M.D. (1987). Human engineering and software maintainability effects on software reliability. *Proc. Ann. Reliability and Maintainability Symp.*, pp.374-377.

Hansen, M.D. and Watts, R.L. (1988). Software system safety and reliability. *Proc. Ann. Reliability and Maintainability Symp.*, pp.214-217.

Harris, L.N. (1986). Software reliability modelling - prospects and perspective. In *Software Reliability: State of the Art Report*, Eds. A. Bendell and P. Mellor, Pengamon Infotech Ltd., pp.105-118.

Harris, L.N. (1987). The use of models in reliability. In *Software Reliability: Achievement and Assessment*, Ed. B. Littlewood, Blackwell, Oxford, pp.167-171.

Haugk, G. et al. (1964). System testing of the No.1 electronic switching system. *The Bell System Technical Journal*, 9, 2575-2592.

Hecht, H. and Hecht, M. (1986). Software reliability in the system context. *IEEE Trans. Software Eng.*, SE-12, 51-58.

Helyer, P. and Davies, C. (1990). Quantitative and qualitative reliability assessment of system including software. *11th Adv. in Reliability Technology Symp.*, April 18-20, Liverpool, London, pp.157-168.

Hennell, M.A. (1991). Testing for the achievement of software reliability. *Reliability Eng. and System Safety*, 32, 119-134.

Higgins, J.J. and Tsokos, C.P. (1981). A quasi-Bayes estimate of the failure intensity of a reliability growth model. *IEEE Trans. Reliability*, R-30, 471-475.

Hirayama, M. et al. (1990). Practice of quality modeling and measurement on software life-cycle. *Proc. 12th Int. Conf. on Software Eng.*, pp.98-107.

Hishitani, J. et al. (1990). Comparison of two estimation methods of the mean time-interval between software failures. *Proc. Int. Phoenix Conf. on Computers and Communications*, pp. 418-424.

Ho, T.F. et al. (1989). A module-structure software reliability model. *Proc. 5th IASTEAD Conf. on Reliability and Quality Control*, June 20-24, Lugano, Switzerland.

Horigome, M. and Kaise, T. (1990). Bayes empirical Bayes models for software reliability and their characteristics. *Proc. Int. Symp. on Reliability and Maintainability*, June 5-8, Tokyo, pp.473-478.

Horigome, M. et al. (1985). A Bayes empirical Bayes approach for (software) reliability growth. In *Computer Science and Statistics*, (16th Symp. Interface, Atlanta, GA, 1984), North-Holland, pp.47-55.

Hsia, P. (1984). Software reliability - theory and practice. *Computer and Electronic Engineering*, 11, 145-149.

Hsieh, M.C. and Iyer, R.K. (1987). A measurement-based model of software reliability in a production environment. *COMPSAC'87*, pp.340-346.

Huang, X.Z. (1984). The hypergeometric distribution model for predicting the reliability of softwares. *Microelectronics and Reliability*, 24, 11-20.

Huang, X.Z. (1985). The new applications of the hypergeometric distribution model on software reliability. *Microelectronics and Reliability*, 25, 713-714.

Huang, X.Z. (1990). The limit condition of some time between failure models of software reliability. *Microelectronics and Reliability*, 30, 481-485.

Hudson, G.R. (1967). Programming errors as a birth-death process. *System Development Corp. Report*, SP-3011.

Iannino, A. et al. (1984). Criteria for software reliability model comparisons. *IEEE Trans. Software Eng.*, SE-10, 687-691.

Jacoby, R. and Tohma, Y. (1990). The hyper-geometric distribution software reliability growth model (HGDM): precise formulation and applicability. *COMPSAC'90*, pp.13-19.

Jacoby, R. and Tohma, Y. (1991). Parameter value computation by least square method and evaluation of software availability and reliability at service-operation by the hyper-geometric distribution software reliability growth model (HGDM). *Proc. 13th Int. Conf. on Software Eng.*, pp.226-237.

Jelinski, Z. and Moranda, P.B. (1972). Software reliability research. In *Statistical Computer Performance Evaluation*, Ed. W. Freiberger, Academic Press, New York, pp.465-497.

Jewell, W.S. (1985). Bayesian extensions to a basic model of software reliability. *IEEE Trans. Software Eng.*, SE-11, 1465-1471.

Jewell, W.S. (1986). Bayesian estimation of undetected errors. In *Theory of Reliability*, Eds. A. Serra and R.E. Barlow, North-Holland, pp.405-425.

Joe, H. (1989). Statistical inference for general-order-statistics and NHPP software reliability models. *IEEE Trans. Software Eng.*, SE-15, 1485-1491.

Joe, H. and Reid, N. (1985a). On the software reliability models of Jelinski-Moranda and Littlewood. *IEEE Trans. Reliability*, R-34, 216-218.

Joe, H. and Reid, N. (1985b). Estimating the number of faults in a system. *J. American Statistical Association*, 80, 222-226.

Jones, W.D. (1991). Reliability models for very large software systems in industry. *Proc. Int. Symp. on Software Reliability Eng.*, pp.35-42.

Kanoun, K. and Sabourin, T. (1987). Failure analysis and operational reliability evaluation in automatic telephone switching software. *Technology and Science of Informatics*, 6, 497-512.

Kanoun, et al. (1991). A method for reliability analysis and prediction application to the TROPICO-R switching system. *IEEE Trans. Software Eng.*, SE-17, 334-344.

Kapur, P.K. and Bhalla, V.K. (1991). Optimal release policies for a flexible software reliability growth model. *Reliability Eng. and System Safety*, to appear.

Kapur, P.K. and Garg, R.B. (1989). Cost-reliability optimum release policies for a software system under penalty cost. *Int. J. Systems Science*, 20, 2547-2562.

Kapur, P.K. and Garg, R.B. (1990a). Cost-reliability optimum release policies for a software system with testing effort. *OPSEARCH*, 27, 109-114.

Kapur, P.K. and Garg, R.B. (1990b). Optimal software release policies for software reliability growth models under imperfect debugging. *Operations Research*, 24, 295-305.

Kapur, P.K. and Garg, R.B. (1991a). Optimum release policy for inflection S-shaped software reliability growth model. *Microelectronics and Reliability*, 31, 39-42.

Kapur, P.K. and Garg, R.B. (1991b). Optimal software release policies for software reliability growth models under imperfect debugging. *R.A.I.R.O.*, to appear.

Kareer, N. et al. (1990). An S-shaped software reliability growth model with two types of errors. *Microelectronics and Reliability*, 30, 1085-1090.

Keene, S.J. (1991a). Cost effective software quality. *Proc. Ann. Reliability and Maintainability Symp.*, pp.433-437.

Keene, S.J. (1991b). Software reliability directions. *Reliability Review*, 11, 3-6.

Keiller, P.A. and Miller, D.R. (1991). On the use and the performance of software reliability growth. *Reliability Eng. and System Safety*, 32, 95-117.

Keiller, P.A. et al. (1983). On the quality of software reliability predictions. In *Electronic Systems Effectiveness and Life Cycle Costing*, Ed. J.K. Skwirzynski, NATO ASI Series, Vol.F22, Springer-Verlag, Berlin, pp.441-460.

Kenett, R. and Pollak, M. (1986). A semi-parametric approach to testing for reliability growth, with application to software systems. *IEEE Trans. Reliability*, R-35, 304-310.

Khoshgoftaar, T.M. (1988). Nonhomogeneous Poisson processes for software reliability growth. *COMPSTAT'88*, Copenhagen, Denmark, pp.13-14.

Khoshgoftaar, T.M. and Munson, J.C. (1990). Predicting software development errors using software complexity metrics. *IEEE J. Selected Areas in Commun.*, SAC-8, 253-261.

Khoshgoftaar, T.M. and Woodcock, T.G. (1991). Software reliability model selection, a case study. *Proc. Int. Symp. on Software Reliability Eng.*, pp.183-191.

Kitaoka, T. et al. (1986). A discrete non-homogeneous error detection model for software reliability. *Trans. IEICE of Japan*, 69, 859-865.

Kitchenham, B.A. and Littlewood, B. (1989). *Measurement for Software Control and Assurance*. Elsevier, London.

Kline, M.B. (1980). Software and hardware R&M: what are the differences? *Proc. Ann. Reliability and Maintainability Symp.*, pp.179-183.

Knafl, G.J. and Sacks, J. (1991). Poisson processes with nearly constant failure intensity. *Proc. Int. Symp. on Software Reliability Eng.*, pp.60-66.

Knight, J.C. and Ammann, P.E. (1985). An experimental evaluation of simple methods for seeding program errors. *Proc. 7th Int. Conf. on Software Eng.*, pp.337-342.

Koch, G. and Spreij, P.J.C. (1983). Software reliability as an application of martingale & filtering theory. *IEEE Trans. Reliability*, R-32, 342-345.

Koch, H.S. and Kubat, P. (1983). Optimal release time of computer software. *IEEE Trans. Software Eng.*, SE-9, 323-327.

Komuro, Y. (1987). Evaluation of software products´ testing phase - application to software reliability growth models. In *Reliability Theory and Applications*, Eds. S. Osaki and J. Cao, World Scientific, Singapore, pp.188-194.

Koss, W.E. (1988). Software reliability metrics for military systems. *Proc. Ann. Reliability and Maintainability Symp.*, pp.190-194.

Kremer, W. (1983). Birth-death and bug counting. *IEEE Trans. Reliability*, R-32, 37-47.

Kruger, G.A. (1988). Project management using software reliability growth models. *Hewlett-Packard Journal*, 39, 30-35.

Kubat, P. (1989). Assessing reliability of modular software. *Operations Research Letters*, 8, 35-41.

Kubat, P. and Koch, H.S. (1983a). Managing test-procedures to achieve reliable software. *IEEE Trans. Reliability*, R-32, 299-303.

Kubat, P. and Koch, H.S. (1983b). Pragmatic testing protocols to measure software reliability. *IEEE Trans. Reliability*, R-32, 338-341.

Kumar, V.K.P. et al. (1986). Distributed program reliability analysis. *IEEE Trans. Software Eng.*, SE-12, 42-50.

Kuo, W. (1983). Software reliability estimation: a realization of competing risk. *Microelectronics and Reliability*, 23, 249-260.

Kyparisis, J. and Singpurwalla, N.D. (1985). Bayesian inference for the Weibull process with applications to assessing software reliability growth and predicting software failures. In *Computer Science and Statistics*, (16th Symp. Interface, Atlanta, GA, 1984), North-Holland, pp.57-64.

Langberg, N. and Singpurwalla, N.D. (1985). A unification of some software reliability models. *SIAM J. Scientific and Statistical Computation*, 6, 781-790.

Langberg, N. and Singpurwalla, N.D. (1986). Some foundation consideration in software reliability modelling and a unification of some software reliability models. In *Theory of Reliability*, Eds. A. Serra and R.E. Barlow, North-Holland, Amsterdam, pp.321-378.

Laprie, J.C. (1984). Dependability modeling and evaluation of software and hardware systems. *Proc. Int. Conf. on Fault-Tolerant Computing*, pp.202-215.

Le Gall, G. and Derriennic, H. (1990). An experiment in using conventional software reliability growth models in telecommunications. *Proc. Int. Symp. on Reliability and Maintainability*, June 5-8, Tokyo, pp.283-288.

Lennselius, B. and Rydström, L. (1990). Software fault content and reliability estimations for telecommunication systems. *IEEE J. Selected Area in Commun.*, SAC-8, 262-272.

Lennselius, B. et al. (1987). Software metrics: fault content estimation and software process control. *Microprocessors and Microsystems*, 11, 365-375.

Leone, A.M. (1988). Selecting on appropriate model for software reliability. *Proc. Ann. Reliability and Maintainability Symp.*, pp.208-213.

Levendel, Y. (1987). Quality and reliability estimation for large software projects using a time-dependent model. *COMPSAC'87*, pp.340-346.

Levendel, Y. (1990). Reliability analysis of large software systems: defect data modeling. *IEEE Trans. Software Eng.*, SE-16, 141-152.

Leveson, N.G. and Harvey, P.R. (1983). Software fault tree analysis. *J. Systems and Software*, 3, 173-181.

Levin, K.D. and Yadid, O. (1990). Optimal release time of improved versions of software packages. *Information and Software Techn.*, 32, 65-70.

Lin, H.H. and Kuo, W. (1987). Reliability cost in software life-cycle models. *Proc. Ann. Reliability and Maintainability Symp.*, pp.364-346.

Lipaev, V.I. (1986). Software reliability, a review of the concepts. *Automation and Remote Control*, 47, 1313-1335.

Lipow, M. (1978). Models for software reliability. *J. American Society of Mechanical Engineers*, 1, 1-11.

Lipow, M. (1982). Number of faults per line of code. *IEEE Trans. Software Eng.*, SE-8, 437-440.

Lipow, M. (1985). A new approach to software reliability. *Proc. Ann. Reliability and Maintainability Symp.*, pp.262-266,

Lipow, M. and Thayer, T.A. (1977). Prediction of software failures. *Proc. Ann. Reliability and Maintainability Symp.*, pp.489-494.

Littlewood, B. (1975). A reliability model for systems with Markov structure. *Applied Statistics*, 24, 172-177.

Littlewood, B. (1979a). How to measure software reliability and how not to. *IEEE Trans. Reliability*, R-28, 103-110.

Littlewood, B. (1979b). Software reliability model for modular program structure. *IEEE Trans. Reliability*, R-28, 241-246.

Littlewood, B. (1980a). The Littlewood-Verrall model for software reliability compared with some rivals. *J. Systems and Software*, 1, 251-258.

Littlewood, B. (1980b). Theory of software reliability: how good are they and how they can be improved? *IEEE Trans. Software Eng.*, SE-6, 489-500.

Littlewood, B. (1981a). Stochastic reliability-growth: a model for fault-removal in computer-programs and hardware-designs. *IEEE Trans. Reliability*, R-30, 313-320.

Littlewood, B. (1981b). A critique of the Jelinski-Moranda model for software reliability. *Proc. Ann. Reliability and Maintainability Symp.*, pp.357-361.

Littlewood, B. (1984). Rationale for a modified Duane model. *IEEE Trans. Reliability*, R-33, 157-159.

Littlewood, B. (1987a). *Software Reliability: Achievement and Assessment*. Blackwell, Oxford.

Littlewood, B. (1987b). How good are software reliability predictions. In *Software Reliability: Achievement and Assessment*. Ed. B. Littlewood, Blackwell, Oxford, pp.172-191.

Littlewood, B. (1988). Forecasting software reliability. In *Software Reliability Modelling and Identification*, Ed. S. Bittanti, Springer-Verlag, Berlin, pp.141-209.

Littlewood, B. (1989). Predicting software reliability. *Phil. Trans. R. Soc. London - A*, 327, 513-527.

Littlewood, B. and Miller, D.R. (1989). Conceptual modeling of coincident failures in multiversion software. *IEEE Trans. Software Eng.*, SE-15, 1596-1614.

Littlewood, B. and Sofer, A. (1987). A Bayesian modification to the Jelinski-Moranda software reliability growth model. *Software Engineering J.*, 2, 30-41.

Littlewood, B. and Verrall, J.L. (1973). A Bayesian reliability growth model for computer software. *Applied Statistics*, 22, 332-346.

Littlewood, B. and Verrall, J.L. (1981). Likelihood function of a debugging model for computer software reliability. *IEEE Trans. Reliability*, R-30, 145-148.

Littlewood, B. et al. (1986). Tools for the analysis of the accuracy of software reliability predictions. In *Software System Design Methods*, Ed. J.K. Skwirzynski, NATO ASI Series, Vol.F22, Springer-Verlag, Berlin, pp.299-335.

Liu, G. (1987). A Bayesian assessing method of software reliability growth. In *Reliability Theory and Applications*, Eds. S. Osaki and J. Cao, World Scientific, Singapore, pp.237-244.

Liu, T.S. and Howell, T.H. (1984). Survey and application of software reliability models. *Proc. Int. Phoenix Conf. on Computer and Communications*, pp.200-206.

London, R.L. (1969). Proving programs correct: some techniques and examples. *BIT*, 10, 168-182.

Luman, R.L. (1984). Practical Kalman filter software performance testing and validation. *IEEE Trans. Reliability*, R-33, 219-226.

Lyu, M.R. and Nikora, A. (1991). A heuristic approach for software reliability prediction: the equally-weighted linear combination model. *Proc. Int. Symp. on Software Reliability Eng.*, pp.172-181.

Mainini, M.T. and Billot, L. (1990). PERFIDE: an environment for evaluation and monitoring of software reliability metrics during the test phase. *Software Engineering J.*, 5, 27-32.

Marriott, (1987). How to plan and manager the reliability of software - a practical approach. *Proc. 5th Int. Conf. on Systems Eng.*, Sept.9-11, Dayton, pp.521-524.

Martini, M.R.B. et al. (1990). Software reliability evaluation of the TROPICO-R switching system. *IEEE Trans. Reliability*, R-39, 369-379.

Masuda, Y. et al. (1989). A statistical approach for determining release time of software system with modular structure. *IEEE Trans. Reliability*, R-38, 365-372.

Matsumoto, K. et al. (1988). Experimental evaluation of software reliability growth models. *Proc. Int. Conf. on Fault-Tolerant Computing*, pp.148-156.

Mazzuchi, T.A. and Soyer, R. (1988). A Bayes empirical-Bayes model for software reliability. *IEEE Trans. Reliability*, R-37, 248-254.

McCall, T. (1976). A complexity measure. *IEEE Trans. Software Eng.*, SE-2, 308-320.

McCollin, C. et al. (1989). Effects of explanatory factors on software reliability. *RELIABILITY'89*, paper 5Ba/1.

Meinhold, R.J. and Singpurwalla, N.D. (1983). Bayesian analysis of a commonly used model for describing software failures. *The Statistician*, 32, 168-173.

Mellor, P. (1984). Analysis of software failure data: adaptation of the Littlewood stochastic reliability growth model for coarse data. *ICL Technical J.*, 4, 159-194.

Mellor, P. (1986). Software reliability data collection: problems and standards. In *Software Reliability: State of the Art Report*, Eds. A. Bendell and P. Mellor, Pengamon Infotech Ltd., pp.165-181.

Mellor, P. (1987a). Experiments in software reliability estimation. *Reliability Eng.*, 18, 117-129.

Mellor, P. (1987b). Software reliability modelling: the state of the art. *Information and Software Techn.*, 29, 81-98.

Miller, D.R. (1986). Exponential order statistic models of software reliability growth. *IEEE Trans. Software Eng.*, SE-12, 12-24.

Miller, D.R. and Sofer, A. (1985). Completely monotone regression estimates of software failure rates. *Proc. 8th Int. Conf. on Software Eng.*, pp.343-348.

Miller, D.R. and Sofer, A. (1986). A non-parametric approach to software reliability, using complete monotonicity. In *Software Reliability: State of the Art Report*, Eds. A. Bendell and P. Mellor, Pengamon Infotech Ltd., pp.19-29.

Misra, P.N. (1983). Software reliability analysis. *IBM Systems J.*, 22, 262-270.

Moranda, P.B. (1975). Prediction of software reliability during debugging. *Proc. Ann. Reliability and Maintainability Symp.*, pp.327-332.

Moranda, P.B. (1981). An error detection model for application during software development. *IEEE Trans. Reliability*, R-30, 309-315.

Munson, J.C. and Khoshgoftaar, T.M. (1990a). Regression modelling of software quality: empirical investigation. *Information and Software Techn.*, 32, 106-114.

Munson, J.C. and Khoshgoftaar, T.M. (1990b). The relative software complexity metric: a validation study. *Proc. 12th Inf. Conf. on Software Eng.*, pp.89-102.

Munson, J.C. and Khoshgoftaar, T.M. (1991). The use of software complexity metrics in software reliability modeling. *Proc. Int. Symp. on Software Reliability Eng.*, pp.2-11.

Musa, J.D. (1975). A theory of software reliability and its application. *IEEE Trans. Software Eng.*, SE-1, 312-327.

Musa, J.D. (1979a). *Software Reliability Data*. Report available from Data and Analysis Center for Software, Rome Air Development Center, New York.

Musa, J.D. (1979b). Validity of the execution time theory of software reliability. *IEEE Trans. Reliability*, R-28, 181-191.

Musa, J.D. (1980). Software reliability measurement. *J. Systems and Software*, 1, 223-241.

Musa, J.D. (1984). Software reliability. In *Handbook of Software Engineering*, Eds. C.R. Vick and C.V. Ramamoorthy, pp.392-412.

Musa, J.D. (1987). Software quality and reliability basics. *Proc. Computer Conf.*, Dallas, Oct.25-29, pp.114-115.

Musa, J.D. (1988). Introduction to software reliability. *Technology and Science of Information*, 6, 483-495.

Musa, J.D. and Ackerman, A.F. (1989). Quantifying software validation: when to stop testing? *IEEE Software*, 2, 19-22.

Musa, J.D. and Okumoto, K. (1983). Software reliability models: concepts, classification, comparisons, and practice. In *Electronic Systems Effectiveness and Life Cycle Costing*, Ed. J.K. Skwirzynski, NATO ASI Series, Vol.3, Springer-Verlag, Berlin, pp.441-460.

Musa, J.D. and Okumoto, K. (1984a). A comparison of time domains for software reliability models. *J. Systems and Software*, 4, 277-287.

Musa, J.D. and Okumoto, K. (1984b). A logarithmic Poisson execution time model for software reliability measurement. *Proc. 7th Int. Conf. on Software Eng.*, pp.230-238.

Musa, J.D. and Okumoto, K. (1986). Application of basic and logarithmic Poisson execution time models in software reliability measurement. In *Software System Design Methods*, Ed. J.K. Skwirzynski, NATO ASI Series, Vol.F22, Springer-Verlag, Berlin, pp.275-298.

Musa, J.D. et al. (1987a). *Software Reliability: Measurement, Prediction, Application*. McGraw-Hill, New York.

Musa, J.D. et al. (1987b). Introduction to software reliability. *Technology and Science of Information*, 6, 483-495.

Nakagawa, Y. and Hanata, S. (1989). An error complexity model for software reliability measurement. *Proc. 11th Int. Conf. on Software Eng.*, pp.230-236.

Nathan, I. (1979). A deterministic model to predict "error-free" status of complex software development. In *Workshop on Quantitative Software Models for Software Reliability, Complexity and Cost: An Assessment of the State of the Art*.

Nayak, T.K. (1986). Software reliability: statistical modeling and estimation. *IEEE Trans. Reliability*, R-35, 566-570.

Nelson, E. (1978). Estimating software reliability from test data. *Microelectronics and Reliability*, 17, 67-74.

De Neumann, B. (1987). Entropy/information theory and (software) reliability. In *Software Reliability: Achievement and Assessment*, Ed. B. Littlewood, Blackwell, Oxford, pp.167-171.

Noon, D.W. (1987). Practical software reliability. In *Reliability of Instrumentation Systems*, Eds. J.P. Jansen and L. Boullart, Pergamon, Oxford, pp.89-96.

Ohba, M. (1984). Software reliability analysis models. *IBM J. Research and Development*, 28, 428-443.

Ohba, M. (1987). SPQL: improvement of error seeding method. In *Reliability Theory and Applications*, Eds. S. Osaki and J. Cao, World Scientific, Singapore, pp.294-303.

Ohba, M. and Chou, X.M. (1989). Does imperfect debugging affect software reliability growth? *Proc. 11th Int. Conf. on Software Eng.*, pp.237-244.

Ohba, M. and Yamada, S. (1984). S-shaped software reliability models. *4th Int. Conf. on Reliability and Maintainability*, pp.430-436.

Ohba, M. et al. (1982). S-shaped software reliability growth curve: how good is it? *COMPSAC'82*, pp.38-44.

Ohtera, H. and Yamada, S. (1990). Optimal allocation & control problems for software-testing resources. *IEEE Trans. Reliability*, R-39, 171-176.

Ohtera, H. et al. (1990a). An optimal release problem based on a testing-effort dependent software reliability model. *Trans. IEICE of Japan*, 71, 1140-1145.

Ohtera, H. et al. (1990b). Software reliability growth model with testing-domain and comparisons of goodness-of-fit. *Proc. Int. Symp. on Reliability and Maintainability*, June 5-8, Tokyo, pp.289-294.

Ohtera, H. et al. (1990c). Software availability based on reliability growth models. *Trans. IEICE of Japan*, 73, 1264-1269.

Okumoto, K. (1985). A statistical method for software quality control. *IEEE Trans. Software Eng.*, SE-11, 1424-1430.

Okumoto, K. and Goel, A.L. (1980). Optimum release time for software systems based on reliability and cost criteria. *J. Systems and Software*, 1, 315-318.

Ottenstein, L. (1981). Predicting numbers of errors using software science. *ACM/Sigmetrics*, 10, 157-167.

Pattipati, K.R. and Shah, S.A. (1990). On the computational aspects of performability models of fault-tolerant computer systems. *IEEE Trans. Computers*, C-39, 832-836.

Petrova, E. and Veevers, A. (1990). Role of non-stochastic-based metrics in quantification of software reliability. *Information and Software Techn.*, 32, 71-778.

Raftery, A.E. (1988). Analysis of a simple debugging model. *Applied Statistics*, 37, 12-22.

Raheja, D. (1990). Software system failure mode and effects analysis - a tool for reliability growth. *Proc. Int. Symp. on Reliability and Maintainability*, June 5-8, Tokyo, pp.271-276.

Ramamoorthy, C.V. and Bastani, F.B. (1982). Software reliability - status and perspectives. *IEEE Trans. Software Eng.*, SE-8, 354-371.

Ramamoorthy, C.V. et al. (1975). Reliability and integrity of large computer programs. *Infotech State of the Art Report 20*, pp.617-630.

Ramamoorthy, C.V. et al. (1986). Software reliability: its nature, models and improvement techniques. In *Reliability Theory*, Eds. A. Serra and R.E. Barlow, North-Holland, Amsterdam, pp.287-320.

Reifer, D.J. (1979). Software failure models and effects analysis. *IEEE Trans. Reliability*, R-28, 247-249.

Roca, J.L. (1988). A method for microprocessor software reliability prediction. *IEEE Trans. Reliability*, R-37, 88-90.

Romeu, J.L. and Dey, K.A. (1984). Classifying combined hardware software reliability models. *Proc. Ann. Reliability and Maintainability Symp.*, pp.282-288.

Rook, P. (1990). *Software Reliability Handbook*. Elsevier, London.

Ross, S.M. (1985a). Statistical estimation of software reliability. *IEEE Trans. Software Eng.*, SE-11, 479-483.

Ross, S.M. (1985b). Software reliability: the stopping rule problem. *IEEE Trans. Software Eng.*, SE-11, 1472-1476.

Rubey, R.J. and Harwick, R.D. (1968). Quantitative measurement of program quality. *Proc. of the ACM National Conf.*, pp.671-677.

Rydström, L. and Viktorsson, O. (1989). Software reliability prediction for large and complex telecommunication systems. *Proc. 22nd Ann. Hawaii Int. Conf. on Systems Science*, pp.312-319.

Sandoh, H. and Sawada, K. (1991). Reliability demonstration testing for discrete-type software. *Proc. Ann. Reliability and Maintainability Symp.*, pp.428-432.

Sauter, J.L. (1969). Reliability in computer programs. *Mechanical Engineering*, 91, 24-27.

Schagen, I.P. (1987). A new model for software failure. *Reliability Eng.*, 205-221.

Schagen, I.P. and Sallih, M.M. (1987). Fitting software failure data with stochastic models. *Reliability Eng.*, 17, 111-120.

Scherman, P.S. (1987). How to specify the user's requirements to obtain and verify reliable software for process control applications. In *Reliability of*

Instrumentation Systems, Eds. J.P. Jansen and L. Boullart, Pergamon Press Ltd., Oxford, pp.79-82.

Schick, G.J. and Wolverton, R.W. (1973). Assessment of software reliability. *Proc. Operations Research*, Physica-Verlag, Wurzburg-Wein, pp.395-422.

Schick, G.J. and Wolverton, R.W. (1978). An analysis of competing software reliability models. *IEEE Trans. Software Eng.*, SE-4, 104-120.

Schneider, V. (1981). Some experimental estimators for developmental and developed errors in software development projects. *ACM/Sigmetrics*, 10, 169-171.

Schneidewind, N.F. (1975). Analysis of error processes in computer software. *Sigplan Notices*, 10, 337-346.

Scholz, F.W. (1986). Software reliability modeling and analysis. *IEEE Trans. Software Eng.*, SE-12, 25-31.

Scott, R.K. et al. (1987). Fault-tolerant software reliability modelling. *IEEE Trans. Software Eng.*, SE-13, 582-592.

Selby, R.W. (1990). Empirically based analysis of failures in software systems. *IEEE Trans. Reliability*, R-39, 444-448.

Seth, S.C. et al. (1990). A statistical theory of digital circuit testability. *IEEE Trans. Computers*, C-39, 582-586.

Shanthikumar, J.G. (1981). A general software reliability model for performance prediction. *Microelectronics and Reliability*, 21, 671-682.

Shanthikumar, J.G. (1983). Software reliability models: a review. *Microelectronics and Reliability*, 23, 903-943.

Shanthikumar, J.G. and Tufekci, S. (1983). Application of a software reliability model to decide software release time. *Microelectronics and Reliability*, 23, 41-59.

Sheppard, M. (1990). Early life-cycle metrics and software quality models. *Information and Software Techn.*, 32, 311-316.

Sherif, Y.S. and Kheir, N.A. (1984). Reliability and failure analysis of computing systems. *Computer and Electrical Eng.*, 11, 151-157.

Shooman, M.L. (1972). Probabilistic models for software reliability prediction. In *Statistical Computer Performance Evaluation*, Ed. W. Freiberger, Academic Press, New York, pp.485-502.

Shooman, M.L. (1975). Software reliability: measurement and models. *Proc. Ann. Reliability and Maintainability Symp.*, pp.485-491.

Shooman, M.L. (1983). *Software Engineering: Design, Reliability, and Management*. McGraw-Hill, New York.

Shooman, M.L. (1984). Software reliability: a historical perspective. *IEEE Trans. Reliability*, R-33, 48-55.

Shooman, M.L. (1987a). Reliability of process control software. In *Reliability of Instrumentation Systems*, Eds. J.P. Jansen and L. Boullart, Pergamon Press Ltd., Oxford, pp.21-32.

Shooman, M.L. (1987b). Yes, software reliability can be measured and predicted. *Proc. Computer Conf.*, Dallas, Oct.25-29, pp.121-122.

Shooman, M.L. (1991). A micro software reliability model for prediction and test apportionment. *Proc. Int. Symp. on Software Reliability Eng.*, pp.52-59.

Simkins, D.J. (1983). Software performance modeling and management. *IEEE Trans. Reliability*, R-32, 293-295.

Simmonds, W.H. (1987). Can software reliability be evaluated? In *Reliability of Instrumentation Systems*, Eds. J.P. Jansen and L. Boullart, Pergamon Press Ltd., Oxford, pp.83-88.

Singpurwalla, N.D. and Soyer, R. (1987). Assessing (software reliability growth using a random coefficient autoregressive process and its ramifications. *IEEE Trans. Software Eng.*, SE-11, 1456-1464.

Soi, I.M. and Gopal, K. (1980). Hardware vs software reliability - a comparative study. *Microelectronics and Reliability*, 20, 881-885.

Soyer, R. (1986). Applications of time series models to software reliability analysis. In *Software Reliability: State of the Art Report*, Eds. A. Bendell and P. Mellor, Pengamon Infotech Ltd., pp.197-208.

Spreij, P. (1985). Parameter estimation for a specific software reliability model. *IEEE Trans. Reliability*, R-34, 323-328.

Strandberg, K. and Andersson, H. (1982). On a model for performance prediction. *Microelectronics and Reliability*, 22, 227-240.

Stålhane, T. (1986). Software reliability - a summary of state of the art. *SINTEF REPORT*, No.209, Trondheim, Norway.

Stålhane, T. (1989). Fault tree analysis applied to software. In *Reliability Achievement - The Commercial Incentive*, ed. T. Aven, Elsevier, pp.166-178.

Stålhane, T. and Lindqvist, B.H. (1989). A general Markov model for usage dependent software. *RELIABILITY'89*, paper 5Ba/2.

Sugiura, N. et al. (1974). On the software reliability. *Microelectronics and Reliability*, 13, 529-533.

Sukert, A.N. (1977). An investigation of software reliability models. *Proc. Ann. Reliability and Maintainability Symp.*, pp.478-484.

Sukert, A.N. (1979). Empirical validation of three software error prediction models. *IEEE Trans. Reliability*, R-28, 199-205.

Sukert, A. and Goel, A. (1980). A guidebook for software reliability assessment. *Proc. Ann. Reliability and Maintainability Symp.*, pp.186-190.

Sumita, U. and Masuda, Y. (1986). Analysis of software error prediction models. *IEEE Trans. Software Eng.*, SE-12, 32-41.

Sumita, U. and Shanthikumar, J.G. (1986). A software reliability model with multiple-error introduction and removal. *IEEE Trans. Reliability*, R-35, 459-462.

Thayer, T.A. et al. (1978). *Software Reliability*. North-Holland, New York.

Thompson, W.E. and Chelson, P.O. (1980). On the specification and testing of software reliability. *Proc. Ann. Reliability and Maintainability Symp.*, pp.379-383.

Tohma, Y. et al. (1989a). Structural approach to the estimation of the number of residual software faults based on the hypergeometric distribution. *IEEE Trans. Software Eng.*, SE-15, 345-362.

Tohma, Y. et al. (1989b). Hyper-Geometric distribution model to estimate the number of residual software faults. *COMPSAC'89*, pp.610-617.

Tohma, Y. et al. (1991). Parameter estimation of the hyper-geometric distribution model for real test/debugging data. *Proc. Int. Symp. on Software Reliability Eng.*, pp.28-34.

Trachtenberg, M. (1985). The linear software reliability model and uniform testing. *IEEE Trans. Reliability*, R-34, 8-16.

Trachtenberg, M. (1990). A general theory of software reliability modeling. *IEEE Trans. Reliability*, R-39, 92-96.

Trivedi, A. and Shooman, M. (1975). A many-state Markov model for the estimation and prediction of computer software performance parameters. *Proc. 1975 Int. Conf. on Reliable Software*, pp.208-220.

Troy, R. and Moawad, R. (1985). Assessment of software reliability models. *IEEE Trans. Software Eng.*, SE-11, 839-849.

Troy, R. and Romain, Y. (1986). A statistical methodology for the study of the software failure process and its application to the ARGOS Center. *IEEE Trans. Software Eng.*, SE-12, 345-355.

Uemura, M. et al. (1990). Software reliability evaluation method: application of delayed S-shaped NHPP model and other related models. *Proc. Int. Conf. on Reliability and Maintainability*, June 5-8, Tokyo, pp.467-472.

Vallarino, C.R. (1989). Fitting the log-linear rate to Poisson processes. *Proc. Ann. Reliability and Maintainability Symp.*, pp.257-261.

Vallee, F. and Ragot, A. (1991). Reliability evaluation using NHPP models. *Proc. Int. Symp. on Software Reliability Eng.*, pp.157-162.

Veevers, A. et al. (1987). Statistical methods for software reliability assessment: past, present and future. In *Achieving Safety and Reliability with Computer Systems*, Ed. B.K. Daniels, Elsevier, London, pp.131-140.

Vienneau, R.L. (1991). The cost of testing software. *Proc. Ann. Reliability and Maintainability Symp.*, pp.423-427.

Wall, J.K. and Ferguson, P.A. (1977). Pragmatic software reliability prediction. *Proc. Ann. Reliability and Maintainability Symp.*, pp.485-488.

Walls, L.A. and Bendell, A. (1986). An exploratory approach to software reliability measurement. In *Software Reliability: State of the Art Report*, Eds. A. Bendell and P. Mellor, Pengamon Infotech Ltd., pp.209-227.

Weiss, H.K. (1956). Estimation of reliability growth in a complex system with Poisson-type failure. *Operations Research*, 4, 532-545.

Weiss, S.N. and Weyuker, E.J. (1988). An extended domain-based model of software reliability. *IEEE Trans. Software Eng.*, SE-14, 1512-1524.

Wightman, D.W. and Bendell, A. (1986a). Proportional hazards modelling of software failure data. In *Software Reliability: State of the Art Report*, Eds. A. Bendell and P. Mellor, Pengamon Infotech Ltd., pp.229-242.

Wightman, D.W. and Bendell, A. (1986b). The application of proportional hazards modelling. *Reliability Eng.*, 15, 29-53.

Wohlin, C. (1988). Some new aspects on software reliability model comparisons. *Proc. 10th Int. Conf. on Software Eng.*, pp.38-42.

Wohlin, C. and Körner, U. (1990). Software faults: spreading, detection and costs. *Software Engineering J.*, 5, 33-42.

Wright, D.E. and Hazelhurst, C.E. (1988). Estimation and prediction for a simple software reliability model. *The Statistician*, 37, 319-325,

Xie, M. (1987). A shock model for software failures. *Microelectronics and Reliability*, 27, 717-724.

Xie, M. (1989). On a generalization of the JM-model. *RELIABILITY'89*, Paper 5ba/3.

Xie, M. (1990). A Markov process model for software reliability analysis. *Applied Stochastic Models and Data Analysis*, 6, 207-214.

Xie, M. (1991). On the determination of optimum software release time. *Proc. Int. Symp. on Software Reliability Eng.*, pp.218-224.

Xie, M. and Bergman, B. (1988). On modelling reliability growth for software. *Proc. 8th IFAC Symp. on Identification and System Parameter Estimation*, Aug.27-31, Beijing, China.

Xie, M. and Xu, R. (1989). Combining test strategy in reliability modelling. *Proc. Conf. on Reliability Mathematics*, Sept.17-19, Xian, China.

Xie, M. and Åkerlund, O. (1989). Applications of software reliability models - possible problems and practical solutions. In *Reliability Achievement - The Commercial Incentive*, ed. T. Aven, Elsevier, pp.158-165.

Yaacob, M. and Hartley, M.G. (1981). A survey of microprocessor software reliability with an illustrative example. *Int. J. Electrical Eng. and Education*, 18, 159-174.

Yamada, S. and Ohtera, H. (1990). Software reliability growth models for testing-effort control. *European J. Operations Research*, 46, 343-349.

Yamada, S. and Osaki, S. (1983a). Reliability growth models for hardware and software systems based on nonhomogeneous Poisson processes: a survey. *Microelectronics and Reliability*, 23, 91-112.

Yamada, S. and Osaki, S. (1983b). S-shaped software reliability growth model with four types of software error data. *Int. J. Systems Science*, 14, 683-692.

Yamada, S. and Osaki, S. (1984). Nonhomogeneous error detection rate models for software reliability growth. In *Stochastic Models in Reliability Theory*, Eds. S. Osaki and Y. Hatoyama, Springer-Verlag, Berlin, pp.129-143.

Yamada, S. and Osaki, S. (1985a). Cost-reliability optimal release policies for software systems. *IEEE Trans. Reliability*, R-34, 422-424.

Yamada, S. and Osaki, S. (1985b). Discrete software reliability growth models. *Applied Stochastic Models and Data Analysis*, 1, 65-77.

Yamada, S. and Osaki, S. (1985c). Software reliability growth modeling: models and applications. *IEEE Trans. Software Eng.*, SE-11, 1431-1437.

Yamada, S. and Osaki, S. (1986). Optimal software release policies for a non-homogeneous software error detection rate model. *Microelectronics and Reliability*, 26, 691-702.

Yamada, S. and Osaki, S. (1987a). Optimal software release policies with simultaneous cost and reliability requirements. *European J. Operations Research*, 31, 46-51.

Yamada, S. and Osaki, S. (1987b). A generalized discrete software reliability growth model and its application. In *Reliability Theory and Applications*, Eds. S. Osaki and J. Cao, World Scientific, Singapore, pp.411-421.

Yamada, S. et al. (1983). S-shaped reliability growth modeling for software error detection. *IEEE Trans. Reliability*, R-32, 475-478.

Yamada, S. et al. (1984a). Software reliability analysis based on a nonhomogeneous error detection rate model. *Microelectronics and Reliability*, 24, 915-920.

Yamada, S. et al. (1984b). Optimum release policies for a software system with a scheduled software delivery time. *Int. J. Systems Science*, 15, 905-914.

Yamada, S. et al. (1984c). S-shaped software reliability growth models and their applications. *IEEE Trans. Reliability*, R-33, 289-292.

Yamada, S. et al. (1985). A software reliability growth model with two types of errors. *R.A.I.R.O.*, 19, 87-104.

Yamada, S. et al. (1986a). Nonhomogeneous software error detection rate model: data analysis and applications. *R.A.I.A.O.*, 20, 51-60.

Yamada, S. et al. (1986b). Software reliability growth models with testing effort. *IEEE Trans. Reliability*, R-35, 19-23.

Yamada, S. et al. (1986c). Discrete models for software reliability evaluation. In *Reliability and Quality Control*, Ed. A.P. Basu, Elsevier, London, pp.401-412.

Yates, W.D. and Shaller, D.A. (1990). Reliability engineering as applied to software. *Proc. Ann. Reliability and Maintainability Symp.*, pp.425-429.

Yu, T.J. et al. (1988). An analysis of several software defect models. *IEEE Trans. Software Eng.*, SE-14, 1261-1267.

Yun, W.Y. and Bai, D.S. (1990). Optimum software release policy with random life cycle. *IEEE Trans. Reliability*, R-39, 167-170.

Zaki, M. and Ei-Boraey, M.M. (1988). Analysis of software reliability models for interconnecting MIMD systems. *J. Systems and Software*, 8, 133-144.

Zeitler, D. (1991). Realistic assumption for software reliability models. *Proc. Int. Symp. on Software Reliability Eng.*, pp.67-74.

Index